Why Play?

Why Play?

How to Make Play an Essential Part of Early Education

Rae Pica

TEACHERS COLLEGE PRESS
TEACHERS COLLEGE | COLUMBIA UNIVERSITY
NEW YORK AND LONDON

Published by Teachers College Press,® 1234 Amsterdam Avenue, New York, NY 10027

Copyright © 2024 by Rae Pica

Cover photos by (clockwise from top left): Maxim Ibragimov, Pratan Ounpitipong, Robert Kneschke, Ground Picture, GUNDAM_Ai, Krisda Ponchaipulltawee, CURIOUs DADA, and Krakenimages.com, all via Shutterstock.

All rights reserved. No part of this publication may be reproduced or transmitted in any form or by any means, electronic or mechanical, including photocopy, or any information storage and retrieval system, without permission from the publisher. For reprint permission and other subsidiary rights requests, please contact Teachers College Press, Rights Dept.: tcpressrights@tc.columbia.edu

Library of Congress Cataloging-in-Publication Data

Names: Pica, Rae, 1953– author.
Title: Why play? : how to make play an essential part of early education / Rae Pica.
Description: New York, NY : Teachers College Press, 2024. |
  Includes bibliographical references and index.
Identifiers: LCCN 2024016279 (print) | LCCN 2024016280 (ebook) |
  ISBN 9780807786208 (paperback) | ISBN 9780807786215 (hardcover) |
  ISBN 9780807782644 (epub)
Subjects: LCSH: Play. | Early childhood education. | Child development.
Classification: LCC LB1139.35.P55 P49 2024 (print) | LCC LB1139.35.P55
  (ebook) | DDC 372.21—dc23/eng/20240611
LC record available at https://lccn.loc.gov/2024016279
LC ebook record available at https://lccn.loc.gov/2024016280

ISBN 978-0-8077-8620-8 (paper)
ISBN 978-0-8077-8621-5 (hardcover)
ISBN 978-0-8077-8624-4 (ebook)

Printed on acid-free paper
Manufactured in the United States of America

*To Nathan Hansen, with love and gratitude for the energy
and enthusiasm that helped me complete this project*

Contents

Acknowledgments	xi
Introduction	1
1. Free Play	**5**
Why Free Play?	5
Putting Theory Into Practice	8
Recommended Resources	10
2. Guided Play	**13**
What Is Guided Play?	13
Why Guided Play?	15
Putting Theory Into Practice	16
Recommended Resources	20
3. Big Body Play	**22**
Why Aren't Children Moving?	22
Why Big Body Play?	24
Putting Theory Into Practice	25
Recommended Resources	28
4. Outdoor Play	**30**
Why Outdoor Play?	31
Why Recess?	33
Putting Theory Into Practice	34
Recommended Resources	37

5.	**Nature Play**	39
	Why Nature Play?	40
	Putting Theory Into Practice	42
	Recommended Resources	44
6.	**Risky Play**	46
	Why Risky Play?	48
	Putting Theory Into Practice	50
	Recommended Resources	52
7.	**Rough-and-Tumble Play**	54
	Why Rough-and-Tumble Play?	55
	Putting Theory Into Practice	56
	Recommended Resources	59
8.	**Cooperative Play**	61
	Is It Really a Dog-Eat-Dog World?	62
	Why Cooperative Play?	63
	Putting Theory Into Practice	65
	Recommended Resources	69
9.	**Dramatic Play**	70
	Why Dramatic Play?	71
	War, Gun, and Superhero Play	72
	Putting Theory Into Practice	73
	Recommended Resources	74
10.	**Fine Motor Play**	76
	Fine Motor Development	77
	Why Fine Motor Play?	78
	Putting Theory Into Practice	79
	Recommended Resources	82

11.	**Construction Play**	**84**
	Why Construction Play?	84
	Putting Theory Into Practice	86
	Recommended Resources	87
12.	**Loose Parts Play**	**89**
	Why Loose Parts Play?	89
	Putting Theory Into Practice	91
	Recommended Resources	93

Conclusion	**95**
References	**97**
Index	**105**
About the Author	**116**

Acknowledgments

So many people have been part of the creation of this book, in both direct and indirect ways.

First and foremost, I must give a great big thank you to my wonderful editor, Sarah Jubar. I knew when she approached me about writing a book on play that working with her would be a fantastic experience. It's one of the reasons I chose to tackle yet another book—and I'm happy to say I was right. Sarah was fun and insightful and so very encouraging.

Of course, I can't fail to give a shout-out to Lenore Skenazy, founder of Free-Range Kids, who pointed me in the direction of Sarah in the first place. Thank you for thinking of me!

Friends and family members offer me love and support in many different ways, but all of them contribute to my ability to do what I do. Much gratitude to Paul Earhart, Sheila Chapman, Patti Page, Jody Martin, Kelly O'Meara, Nicole Parent, Gail Multop, Laura Roush, Leah Moakley (and Patrick, Jack, and Sammy), Sally Haughey, Stephen Pica, and Linda Gladstone Pica. I lost my beloved cat, Mickey, in April of this year, but I have to acknowledge the 15 years of love and laughs he gave me. He made my life so much richer, and his efforts at serving as my "executive assistant" were hilarious and precious. He was the fur love of my life.

Last but certainly not least, I offer my thanks to everyone at Teachers College Press. Special thanks to Abby Naqvi, marketing and sales director; Emily Freyer, digital marketing manager; Alyssa Jordan, editorial assistant; senior production editor Lori Tate; copyeditor Bernadette Malavarca; and director Jennifer Feldman. Dave Strauss, I love the cover you designed! What a wonderful experience working with Teachers College Press has been!

Introduction

What a world our children live in!
When I began working as a consultant in early childhood education more than 4 decades ago, I never could have imagined some of the issues that are now common. From early childhood professionals across the country, and even internationally, I hear that today's young children

- have so little fine motor control that they can't tear a piece of paper;
- are increasingly unable to cross the midline of the body, the invisible vertical line that divides us into left and right sides;
- can't walk a block without becoming exhausted;
- don't have enough core strength to hold themselves upright;
- are falling out of their seats in school; and
- do not know how to play anymore!

All these issues are appalling. But the final one is mind-boggling. How can children be unable to do something they were born to do? Humans—most mammals, in fact—have a biological drive to play (National Institute for Play, n.d.). It's hardwired into them, as is the need to eat, sleep, and breathe.

The sad truth is that children are being allowed so little time to engage in play that they're losing a skill that should inherently be part of them—something through which nature intended them to learn about themselves and the world around them. Although the words are rarely said aloud, *productivity* and *achievement* have come to be valued above free time, even in early childhood. Play is too often viewed as frivolous and unproductive—an attitude prevalent in both homes and learning environments and fueled by such myths as "earlier is better" and "children learn by sitting."

All the problems in the above list can be attributed to too little free time and too little play and movement in children's lives. Why have children become so sedentary? There are several factors involved. One is that parents and policymakers have fallen prey to the above-mentioned myths, which have led to an overemphasis on academics, even among our littlest humans. The result is that early learning and care programs too often neglect the body in favor of the mind, failing to realize the interconnectedness of the two.

Parents have also fallen prey to our culture of fear. They're receiving so many frightening messages—from everywhere—that they're afraid to let their children go outside, lest they become a victim of "stranger danger," an issue even the National Center for Missing and Exploited Children say is a myth (McBride, 2011). Additionally, parents are afraid their children will physically get hurt; even bumps and bruises seem to be considered unacceptable these days. And parents are afraid that if they don't get their little ones started in academics and athletics as early as possible, they will fall behind. The result is that children's days are overscheduled with organized activities their parents have chosen, most of which involve little strenuous engagement. (Even when the organized activity involves a sport, think about the child waiting a turn during T-ball or sitting on the bench during peewee football.) And children as young as preschoolers are expected to do homework nowadays, despite the amount of research indicating it has no value prior to and in elementary school (Kohn, 2007).

This lack of free time has had multiple repercussions for the little ones. Peter Gray (2010) attributes the rise in children's anxiety and depression to the decline of play in their lives. He writes,

> . . . children's freedom to play and explore on their own, independent of direct adult guidance and direction, has declined greatly in recent decades. . . . By depriving children of opportunities to play on their own, away from direct adult supervision and control, we are depriving them of opportunities to learn how to take control of their own lives. We may think we are protecting them, but in fact we are diminishing their joy, diminishing their sense of self-control, preventing them from discovering and exploring the endeavors they would most love, and increasing the odds that they will suffer from anxiety, depression, and other disorders.

It's heartbreaking to have to report that children have even *less* play in their lives since Dr. Gray wrote those words.

The children are suffering. But so, too, are early childhood educators and the profession itself! When I entered the field and traveled the country as a speaker, I rarely heard about burnout among preschool and kindergarten teachers. I did not receive emails from educators and parents distraught because recess had been eliminated at their school. Or because children as young as *one* were expected to sit for extended periods memorizing alphabet and number flashcards. Or because 3-year-olds, whose hands have not yet progressed through the developmental stages necessary for writing, were nevertheless expected to grasp a pencil properly.

Back then, early childhood professionals were not quitting in droves due to the unrealistic expectations placed on them and the children, or due to demands that they teach in ways they *know* to be developmentally inappropriate. But all that has changed over the past couple of decades.

Today, burnout is common among early childhood professionals. Additionally, the field's astonishingly low wages have a direct correlation with the duration of teachers' employment, with some estimates suggesting up to 40% annual turnover in these roles (Tate Sullivan, 2021). And as I was writing this introduction, I came across yet another letter published in a newspaper from a teacher who quit because she simply could not continue. Holly Acre, who taught for 6 years before leaving for a tech job, said, "Before I started teaching, I was a happy-go-lucky person, but over time I noticed teaching was taking that away from me. My day-to-day was unhealthy. I was experiencing burnout and stress, and my body was telling me in no uncertain terms, 'You can't keep doing this.' I was in a state of fight or flight" (Jackson, 2023).

These trends must be reversed! That's why I was compelled to write this book.

Too many of us in the early childhood profession spend an inordinate amount of time defending play. I want to provide you with the information you need—in simple language and an easily digestible format—to champion the return of play to children's lives and education. If we can present our arguments succinctly and with passion, we can help parents, administrators, policymakers, and even other educators see the value of play—to understand its many benefits and realize that young children can learn what they need to know *through play*, as nature intended. When someone witnesses the children playing in your learning environment, I want you to be able to answer the question, "Why are they doing 'this stuff'?"

Each chapter in this book explores a particular type of play. I've chosen to highlight some of the most popular, among them dramatic and loose parts play, but you'll also find chapters on more controversial kinds of play, including "risky" and rough-and-tumble play. They, too, have much to offer children, and we can't allow fear and misconceptions to interfere with children's needs.

Not surprisingly, you'll find an overlap among the different kinds of play. For example, construction play promotes fine motor development. Still, I've chosen to include an individual chapter on fine motor play, as it consists of multiple facets and, despite its importance, is often overlooked in this digital age. Each chapter offers the "why," as well as information you can use to put theory into practice.

I believe it is very important to share information about play with parents, who are receiving so much misinformation via traditional and social media, and from each other. Perhaps the most harmful of that misinformation is the myth that earlier is better. Parents have become deeply committed to the belief that they must give their children the earliest possible start, particularly in academics. It's why they put excessive pressure on early childhood education (ECE) professionals to offer academic-oriented curriculums, as opposed to those that are play-based. Many in the private sector felt they had no choice but to comply; if they didn't, they risked losing enrollment and thus income. The result has been that there are now fewer play-based early learning environments.

Think about what that means in terms of parents' power. If they can bring about a change like that, they can create change in the opposite direction. Moreover, they increase our numbers at the voting booth, which translates to greater power in our advocacy for play and developmentally appropriate practice. For these reasons, each chapter includes a section called "Partnering with Parents." It's my hope these notes will give ECE professionals language they can share with parents to defend play, as well as suggestions for bringing more play to children's home lives. Fortunately, thanks to apps, sharing information with parents is easier these days than ever before.

Those who work with preschoolers and kindergartners (generally children ages 4 to 6) comprise the primary audience for this book. Early childhood encompasses birth through age 8, and as much as I would like to imagine children in first through third grades being availed of the opportunities described in this book, the likelihood of that, sadly, is slim at best. However, should you work with 1st-, 2nd-, or 3rd-graders and have the good fortune to be able to include play in your program, this book is for you as well.

Although you may feel helpless in the face of so much unwanted and unprecedented change in our field, you are not. As I wrote in *Spark a Revolution in Early Education* (Pica, 2023), speaking up empowers you. Having the information you need and sharing your stories about the value of play in children's lives and education can and will make a difference. In fact, our advocacy has already begun to create positive change. According to Blinkoff and colleagues (2023), there is a push to give precedence to play-based learning. Let's keep that push going!

CHAPTER 1

Free Play

Because it encompasses so much—and so many varieties—the word *play* is difficult to define. Many automatically associate play with *games*, a word that can include everything from hopscotch to hockey. Indeed, adults often think of play in terms of competitive sports, even when considering children at play.

But ask a children's play advocate, and most will tell you they believe free play is the only *true* play. That's because free play is child-chosen, child-initiated, and child-directed. The same cannot be said of any organized competitive sport, nor can it be said of such structured activities as gymnastics or ballet, into which millions of young children have been enrolled by adults.

Free play requires no adult involvement at all. It can range from creating art with crayons to creating sound with pots and pans. From running in the backyard to wrestling on the living room floor. It can involve make-believe or making mud pies. It can, in fact, involve nearly all the types of play covered in this book. The focus of free play is the *process*—engagement and enjoyment—and not on such resulting products as a score in a soccer game or even a completed block tower. The tower may be completed, but it is at the child's discretion. Everything—the place, the pace, the plot, the methods, and the materials of the play—is at the discretion of the child or children involved.

WHY FREE PLAY?

To the adult with a checklist of chores, and what the late early childhood educator Bev Bos called "childhood amnesia," there's little purpose to kids donning toy stethoscopes and calling themselves "doctor." There's nothing accomplished when little ones spin in dizzying circles, move empty boxes from one area of the playground to another, or lie on their backs, searching for creatures in the clouds.

Parents intent on their children's success, administrators intent on a school's grades and test scores, and politicians intent on global competition are product- and not process-driven. The majority, I imagine, see little value in free time and *fun*—despite the Declaration of Independence's call for the pursuit of happiness. But fun is what fuels young children. Adults outside of the early childhood profession may not understand this, but those within the profession have *witnessed* it. There's no one more engaged than a child fully absorbed in an undertaking of their own design. That child directs all their concentration and effort—their heart and soul—into whatever has captured their attention. This simply does not happen if the undertaking isn't enjoyable.

In the 1800s, poet Alfred Mercer maintained that what we learn with pleasure we never forget. Music educator Emile Jaques-Dalcroze (1931) later claimed that joy is the most powerful of all mental stimuli. And there's nothing more joyful for children than play. Unfortunately, neither of these men had research to back them up, so it would be difficult for those concerned with academic achievement to trust their contentions. But today, we do have evidence that joy is indeed a necessary component of authentic learning.

A study from two Finnish educators has pointed to several sources of joy in the classroom:

- Active, engaged efforts from the children
- Desire to master the material—to become "expert" at something
- Students allowed to work at their own level and pace
- Finishing a task or solving a problem and the time to do so
- The chance to make choices
- Sharing and collaborating with other students
- The opportunity to play (Rantala and Määttä, 2012)

Additionally, neurologist and educator Judy Willis (2014) tells us, "Joy and enthusiasm are absolutely essential for learning to happen—literally, scientifically, as a matter of fact and research." She attests that when the fun ends, so does the learning. In an earlier work, she wrote,

> The truth is that when we scrub joy and comfort from the classroom, we distance our students from effective information processing and long-term memory storage. Instead of taking pleasure from learning, students become bored, anxious, and anything but engaged. They ultimately learn to feel bad about school and lose the joy they once felt. (Willis, 2007)

The "scrubbing" of joy (i.e., play) from early childhood settings is likely the greatest reason I hear so many stories about young children who were initially excited about "school" but became stressed and miserable within weeks—sometimes days—of attending.

When we offer the doubters justification for free play, we can't forget its role in motivation. The engagement children display through free play is what it means to be *intrinsically motivated*, and intrinsic motivation—the incentive that flows from *within*—is what we want to foster in children. Those asked to pursue external motivation (e.g., blue ribbons, gold stars, or good grades) may find their intrinsic motivation disappearing as the desire for rewards becomes prominent. I often wonder what kind of life it is if extrinsic rewards provide the only incentive for doing something. Why work hard at a project if there's not a promotion involved? Why run the race if you can't be assured of a first-place ribbon? Why volunteer your time and energy if being helpful is the only payoff?

In free play, children discover the pleasure of doing something for its own sake. Also, as they explore and investigate, they recognize their likes and dislikes, strengths and weaknesses, interests and talents. And when children have the chance to choose and spend time on those activities they enjoy—to delve deeper into the possibilities—interests and skills blossom. This is how, as young people and as adults, they find their purpose and passions. The same cannot be said of children whose time and activities are always scheduled for and dictated to them.

But there's even more that children derive from free play. When we watch the child find an original way to keep a block tower from tumbling, or to pretend a fallen log is a rocket ship, we witness children using their imagination, creativity, and problem-solving skills. All of these will serve them well in the future, as problem-solving is necessary in multiple facets of life, and creativity is not the domain of artists alone. We need creativity in business and industry, in science and medicine, in technology, and in education! Moreover, employers are looking for creativity in those they hire. According to a piece in *Forbes*, creativity is the number-one soft skill desired in employees (Blaschka, 2019).

When children participate in free play with others, they develop such essential social skills as negotiation, taking the perspective of others, collaboration, and conflict resolution. They learn to make, follow, and revise rules. All of this contributes to a successful and satisfying place in society. When children participate in free play on their own, they acquire independence, something with which today's young ones have little experience. According to a study from Florida Atlantic University (Anderer, 2023), a lack of independence is having a profound impact on children's mental health. The researchers explain that the "decline over recent decades in opportunities for kids and teens to play, roam, and engage in activities independently" has contributed to "record levels of anxiety, depression, and suicide seen among young people nowadays." They specifically call for more self-directed play and more risk-taking (see Chapter 6 for information on the latter).

It's simply not possible to detail all the benefits of free play here. But the following list from Dr. Michael Patte, a professor of education, sums up the benefits quite nicely:

- It provides opportunities for children to master elements of the world on their own terms.
- It develops self-determination, self-esteem, and the ability to self-regulate—all vital elements of emotional development.
- It fosters social competence, respect for rules, self-discipline, aggression control, problem-solving skills, leadership development, conflict resolution, and playing by the rules.
- It stimulates the senses and allows children to discover the different textures and elements in the world.
- It provides fertile ground to cultivate creativity and imagination.
- It enhances cognitive understandings.
- It builds strength, coordination, and cardiovascular fitness and moderates childhood obesity and its associated health complications.
- It sees boredom as a vehicle for children to create their own happiness, enhance inventiveness, and develop self-reliance (Patte, n.d.).

In *The Brain That Loves to Play: A Visual Guide to Child Development, Play, and Brain Growth*, Dr. Jacqueline Harding (2023) cites research demonstrating that free play is essential to child and brain development. Play, we know, is a biological imperative for children and the way nature intended the little ones to learn. That, I believe, should be all the reason we need to encourage it. After all, how can we possibly imagine we have a better plan than nature's?

PUTTING THEORY INTO PRACTICE

The three most important factors in the encouragement of free play are space, time, and open-ended materials. Although it can be ideal to have a dedicated play center in a classroom, it's not a necessity. We've all witnessed children making magic in a small living room or in something as confined as a sandbox, so it's safe to say children don't require a great deal of space in which to play. However, to allow children the room to play games, act out stories, wrestle, or build as desired, the space you do have available should be *uncluttered*.

Time, of course, is critical to free play. Children *must* have blocks of unscheduled time—the longer, the better—to allow their minds and bodies to roam. And the available materials should be *open-ended*. Possibilities include loose parts, toys, items found in nature, building materials, and other objects that have more than a single use. If children only have access to board games, toy trucks, or talking robots, for example, their play essentially will be prescribed for them, limiting the use of their creativity and imagination. Also, they won't have a chance to practice their problem-solving skills.

Still, even with available space, time, and open-ended materials, you may find there are some children who simply don't know how to engage in free play. They may do nothing at all, or you may witness them repetitively demonstrating the actions of characters they've seen on screens. I'm all for superhero play (see Chapter 10), but it should involve the children's imaginations, which currently don't get enough "exercise" because the many screens in their lives create most of their images for them. If, for instance, you observe children repeatedly thrusting their "light sabers" or performing karate kicks, you'll want to intervene.

Be careful, however, not to let the intervention overtake the children's play. Rather, you can simply ask open-ended questions or present them with challenges. For example, you might ask, "What do you think I should do with these twigs?" You could also join the play briefly, modeling possibilities for them. Denisha Jones, executive director of Defending the Early Years, tells the story of three boys running around the classroom, often interrupting the play of others. Rather than tell them to stop, she moved to the art center, where there were no children playing. When the boys were within hearing distance, she commented on the long strips of paper there, musing that they would make great superhero belts. She then began measuring and decorating the strips. All three boys, along with a girl who'd been in another area, came over to see what Denisha was doing and after some discussion began to play (Jones, 2017).

Your primary role during children's free play is that of observer. In addition to situations such as those described above, you may see that a child is unable to solve a problem and remains stuck. Don't solve the problem for them, but you can scaffold for them. For instance, if a child is having trouble balancing blocks, you could ask, "What do you think would happen if you made the blocks on the bottom cover the biggest space?" Sometimes just describing what you're seeing can help a child find a solution.

Any interventions should be brief. You'll want to step out once the children are engaged, avoiding the temptation to make the play adult-directed and the possibility the children will come to rely on you for what follows.

Remember, too, that observing children at play also helps you better understand each child's development, interests, and strengths. You can then use that knowledge to plan learning experiences and guided play activities for them.

Patte (n.d.) reminds us that recent research has determined children should experience twice as much unstructured play as structured play.

RECOMMENDED RESOURCES

- *Let the Children Play: How More Play Will Save Our Schools and Help Children Thrive* is one of the best books I've read on the subject of play. Written by Pasi Sahlberg and William Doyle, it offers plenty of information to advocate for play.
- If you want support for the role of creativity in a child's future success, I recommend Daniel Pink's *A Whole New Mind: Why Right-Brain Thinkers Will Rule the Future.* Pink contends that it's the artists, storytellers, inventors, and creative right-brain thinkers who will get ahead in the world.
- Pink has also written *Drive: The Surprising Truth About What Motivates Us*. Hint: It is *not* extrinsic rewards.
- I talk with early childhood expert Nancy Carlsson-Paige about children's recent inability to play in this 12-minute podcast episode: https://www.bamradionetwork.com/track/have-children-lost-their-ability-to-play/.

> ### PARTNERING WITH PARENTS
>
> It's essential that parents come to understand the value of free play and how free time, and even boredom, make it possible. If you own a private early learning program, the messaging on your website should make it clear that you value free play. Include photos and videos of children at play—with notes describing what the children are learning—to help promote your philosophy.
>
> Photos and videos can also contribute to emails and newsletters sent to parents. Occasionally, include a quote from someone prominent as "backup" to make parents aware your beliefs are shared by other respected professionals. For instance, Einstein famously said that play is the highest form of research. It's hard to argue with Einstein!
>
> When you have parent-teacher conferences, talk to them from the heart. Clarify that play—*not* tech or worksheets or direct instruction—is the vehicle through which children learn about themselves and the world around them. Gently explain that research has proved that structured activities and screens are among the culprits keeping kids from engaging in as much free play as nature intended them to have. Clarify that open-ended materials are necessary for true play to occur and provide examples. For those who worry about the potential for boredom (young children without adequate downtime often exclaim they're bored when they find themselves idle), recommend that parents keep a list of activities their child enjoys. If their child claims boredom, the parent can present two options from which the child chooses. For example, the child might be given

a choice between finger painting and playing dress-up (with the necessary materials readily available). Parents will want to limit the options to two, as more than that makes it challenging for children to choose.

Asking parents about their own play experiences as children can be a very effective tool. What were their favorite things to do? How much time did they spend playing? What skills did they learn through free play? Reminding them of their own childhoods may help them realize they want the same kind of experiences for their children.

In my presentations, I often ask attendees to imagine trying to keep a kitten or puppy from playing, stressing that it's just as ludicrous to try to keep a young child from playing. I've also been known to show a video of baby goats at play (https://www.youtube.com/watch?v=mtOD19C7J48) to make the point that nature intended the young of almost all species to play. Just as those kids are developing the skills they'll need as adults, so too do human kids develop theirs through play.

Of course, you'll need answers to such frequently asked questions as, "What do you do all day? Are the children just playing all the time?" and "Why aren't you teaching my child anything?" Wunderled's Sara Del Rio offers potential responses in a blog post called "Addressing Parents' Concerns About Play-Based Learning" (https://wunderled.com/blog/addressing-parents-concerns-about-play-based-learning/). In conversations with parents, you can easily adapt Sara's language to match your own style of communication, but this piece is especially helpful to those of us who don't think as quickly as we'd like when asked a controversial question. If you distribute it, be sure to assign proper credit.

It also may be beneficial for parents to know that pediatricians consider play so important that the American Academy of Pediatrics (AAP) has published position statements on the topic. Among them is "The Power of Play: A Pediatric Role in Enhancing Development in Young Children" (https://publications.aap.org/pediatrics/article/142/3/e20182058/38649/The-Power-of-Play-A-Pediatric-Role-in-Enhancing). It's unlikely parents will take the time to read the entire article, but you could create a brief bullet-pointed document for them.

Highlights from the introduction of the article include these points you could share with parents:

- Research demonstrates that developmentally appropriate play with parents and peers is a singular opportunity to promote the social-emotional, cognitive, language, and self-regulation skills that build executive function and a prosocial brain.
- Play supports the formation of the safe, stable, and nurturing relationships with all caregivers that children need to thrive.

- Play is not frivolous: it enhances brain structure and function and promotes executive function, which allow us to pursue goals and ignore distractions.
- When play and safe, stable, nurturing relationships are missing in a child's life, toxic stress can disrupt the development of executive function and the learning of prosocial behavior.
- Play is fundamentally important for learning 21st-century skills, such as problem solving, collaboration, and creativity, which require the executive functioning skills that are critical for adult success.
- A balanced curriculum that includes playful learning is important to child development.

You also may want to share all or part of the *Scientific American* article, "Unstructured Play Is Critical to Child Development" (https://www.scientificamerican.com/article/unstructured-play-is-critical-to-child-development/). Another possibility is the succinctly written "Why Unstructured Free Play Is Important" (https://activeforlife.com/why-unstructured-free-play-is-important/) by Active for Life's Jim Grove.

CHAPTER 2

Guided Play

I once attended a virtual summit in which Kathy Hirsh-Pasek, a champion for young children and co-author of *Einstein Never Used Flashcards*, talked about the value of guided play. I thought her talk was wonderful. So, it came as a huge surprise to me when she received pushback from some play advocates.

Later, I came across a Facebook discussion in which these advocates expressed anger that anyone would recommend anything other than free play. (As you may know, many people believe free play is the only "true" play.) My attempts to clarify Kathy's intentions and defend guided play didn't go over well, but I persisted. I asked, "What about when a teacher arranges a game like Statues, which the children love and that helps foster self-regulation?" The response was, "We don't arrange games." End of discussion.

I'm using this chapter as an opportunity to expand upon the discussion. I offer a description of guided play, as well as examples of this kind of play, and an exploration of its benefits. It's my hope that doubters will come to see guided play's value and the many reasons that, like free play, it should be part of children's lives.

WHAT IS GUIDED PLAY?

Guided play involves learning goals, which makes it more intentional, or purposeful, than free play. It also involves adults, who offer support either *prior* to the play (e.g., by setting up the environment) or *during* the play (e.g., posing questions leading to additional exploration).

Guided play, then, consists of two components: children's autonomy and adult guidance. Weisberg and colleagues (2016) tell us, "Guided play takes advantage of children's natural abilities to learn through play by allowing them to express their autonomy within a prepared environment and with adult scaffolding." To ensure that guided play doesn't become adult-directed, during the play, the children must choose their own actions. Also, the adult guidance must be subtle, allowing the children "to explore the right aspects of the environment to reach the learning goal" (Weisberg and Zoss, 2018).

Some may believe that specifying a learning goal is a direct contradiction to the philosophy of process over product. But a learning goal is not focused on a product (e.g., a completed drawing or block tower). Rather, a learning goal might be focused on the development of self-regulation, problem solving, cooperation, or communication skills. None of these is a product, and the children still direct the learning process.

It is okay to have learning goals for children if they're developmentally appropriate and handled in a way that's respectful to the children. Yes, children learn much from free play. But might they not learn additional skills if we sometimes guide their play? And aren't those additional skills meaningful too?

I often refer to guided play as active—versus passive—learning. Young children are experiential (active) learners who acquire information using multiple senses. The more senses they engage, the more information children absorb and retain. For example, when children move over, under, around, through, beside, and near objects and others, they better grasp the meaning of these prepositions (emergent literacy) and geometry (math) concepts.

Educator and author Eric Jensen (2001) has yet another term for this kind of learning. He refers to it as *intrinsic* (active) learning, such as learning to ride a bike. Jensen uses memorizing the capital of Peru as an example of *extrinsic* (passive) learning. He asks, if you hadn't ridden a bike in 5 years, would you still be able to do it? (Most—if not all—would respond that they could.) And if you hadn't heard the capital of Peru in 5 years, would you still remember it? (I, for one, probably would not.)

Whether it's called guided play, active learning, or intrinsic learning, a teacher who wants children to experience the prepositions and geometry concepts mentioned earlier could offer a worksheet on which the concepts are listed and pictured (passive learning), or the teacher could set up an obstacle course and invite the children to explore it (active learning/guided play). With the latter, to scaffold the learning, the teacher might occasionally point out that the children are moving *through* the tunnel or *under* the rope. In this way, the children are seeing, feeling, and hearing the concepts, making those concepts more meaningful to them.

In yet another example, if the children have discovered a bird's nest in the outdoor play area and express enthusiasm about it, the teacher might ensure there are books about birds and their nests in the reading center. To inspire guided play, she could also make twigs, leaves, dried grass, and plastic eggs and birds available in one area of the classroom. She could prepare the environment for the children's exploration of the topic and could ask an occasional question or make an occasional comment to extend the learning. For instance, as the children are playing with the materials, the teacher might wonder aloud why birds build their nests with such materials as twigs and leaves.

The game Statues, the example given earlier, meets the criteria for guided play because it allows children to move in any way they want while music is playing, and freeze in any way they want when the music pauses. Within that freedom, however, the children engage in active listening (emergent literacy) and practice self-regulation skills (social studies) by halting their movement and holding still. The teacher's role is to select or arrange the environment (perhaps by clearing a space for movement), explain how the game works, and provide and control the music.

I want to issue a caveat here—and it's one that educators often find controversial. I've long believed in giving children *choices*. It provides them with some agency over their lives and helps develop decision-making skills, among others. If guided play is to maintain its integrity and remain developmentally appropriate, the children should have the freedom to choose whether or not they *want* to participate in a particular activity. If we insist that a child explore the nest-making area or take part in a game of Statues, resentment could well be the result—and resentment isn't conducive to learning.

You may worry that giving children so much choice will result in chaos, but it's more likely to result in an environment where the children feel respected and where they will respect you and others in turn—and that *is* conducive to learning.

WHY GUIDED PLAY?

I understand the desire to allow children to learn on their own. I understand the value of free play, as expressed in the previous chapter. However, I can't discount the benefits of guided play. And, really, the argument shouldn't be free versus guided play, but rather guided play versus direct instruction.

To illustrate guided play versus direct instruction, I'll use the game of Statues, again, as an example. Self-regulation, or the ability to understand and manage our own behavior and reactions, can't be imposed by an outside force. Still, some teachers may try to foster it with direct instruction. This often takes the form of an insistence in which children sit still and listen with their "whole bodies." When this fails, a teacher might assume the children can't regulate themselves. However, it simply means they're not yet developmentally ready to sit still (which isn't fun), and the direct instruction offers them little motivation to try.

When children participate in a guided-play game like Statues—or Blast Off, where they crouch low and await the countdown to blast off—they hold still because they *want* to hold still. They're able to regulate themselves because games like Statues and Blast Off are *fun*, which motivates young children.

A recent study (University of Cambridge, 2022) determined that when we have a learning goal in mind, children can learn just as much in some literacy, numeracy, behavioral, and executive-function skills through guided play as they can through direct instruction, or adult-led methods. In some cases—for example, in certain areas of math, like simple computation, the children learn even *more* through guided play. Elizabeth Byrne, a coauthor of the study, believes this is because math concepts can be so abstract, and guided play makes the ideas more concrete for young children. If, for example, children are asked to add two plus three, they would struggle with the abstract thinking involved. But, if the teacher has prepared the environment with manipulatives and asks how many manipulatives they would have if two objects were combined with another three objects, those children familiar with one-to-one correspondence could determine the correct response.

Direct instruction has its place in education, such as when preschool children are taught a song, or when elementary students use rote memorization to learn the multiplication tables, but such practices as the use of worksheets, lectures, skill and drill, and demonstration and imitation are currently being used far too frequently in far too many early learning environments. Not only do teacher-led methods tend to be less enjoyable for children, we know that young children aren't yet ready for abstract thinking. That's why the kind of hands-on learning described in the last section is so essential for them. It makes abstract concepts concrete. As Kathy Hirsh-Pasek has said, it's about teaching "human brains in the way human brains learn" (quoted in Mader, 2022).

Moreover, in direct instruction there is little opportunity for divergent problem solving, in which there are multiple solutions to any single challenge. With guided play, on the other hand, you'll witness children responding in a variety of (sometimes wonderfully surprising) ways to your invitations. For instance, if you're exploring shapes with the children and ask them to show you a crooked shape with their bodies, you're likely to see as many different crooked shapes as there are children! If you ask the children to place five body parts on the floor, one child may count the bottom as one part, while another counts it as two!

Too much traditional schooling gives children the impression that there's only one correct answer to any question, but this is not the way life works. There will never be just one way in which to balance a budget or resolve a conflict. On a larger scale, there will never be a single solution to such issues as poverty or world peace. There will always be problems to solve in life, meaning that divergent problem solving is one skill we *know* children will need wherever their lives take them.

PUTTING THEORY INTO PRACTICE

The activities you choose will depend on your learning goals for the children. For instance, if you want children to experience the scientific concept of flotation, you can make a variety of materials—some that will float and some that will sink—available at the water table. As the children are experimenting, you might ask what they've discovered: "Why do you think the rubber duck floated, but the rock didn't?"

Within the content area of art, you may want children to gain experience with the concept of color. Toward that end, you may choose to make only such art materials as crayons, paints, and squares of cellophane in various colors available in the art center. Then, as you walk among those children engaging with the materials, you may notice some using only one color, and ask what they think would happen if they combined two colors. You're not specifically telling them to mix two colors together; you're simply planting the seed for possible exploration.

If you want to help children explore the artistic concept of texture, you can make such items as feathers, smooth stones, and pieces of bark available. You might ask, "What do you think are the biggest differences between the stone and the bark?"

In math, to help early elementary children learn principles of simple computation, you could place manipulatives such as popsicle sticks or straws on a table. After allowing the children time to experiment, you could group nine sticks or straws together, and ask the children if they can discover other ways to make nine. Possibilities, of course, include groupings of eight and one, six and three, and five and four. Three groups of three is another possibility.

An experiment in sound production, which falls under the content areas of music and emergent literacy (active listening), could involve providing tambourines or rhythm sticks. A possible scaffolding comment in this instance is, "I wonder if you can make two (or three) *different* sounds with the same instrument." Possibilities with a tambourine include shaking it, tapping it with a finger, hitting it with a hand, flicking it with a fingernail, or rubbing it against a body part. You could even hand out sheets of paper and invite the children to discover how many sounds they can create with the paper. Possibilities include tearing it, crumpling it, flicking it with a finger, and even folding it (a quiet sound but a sound nonetheless).

There are many games that can't be included under the heading of guided play because the rules specify exactly how they're to be played. But there are others, a few of which I've already mentioned, that do serve the purposes of guided play. Below are some additional guided-play activities.

 **Shrinking Room**

Learning Goal: Focus on personal space.

Because today's children aren't getting enough movement—particularly the spinning, swinging, upside-down movement that develops the proprioceptive and vestibular senses (see Chapter 3)—many struggle with the concept of personal space. We can (futilely) keep asking children not to bump into one another, or we can help them understand personal space through physical experience.

Prior to playing Shrinking Room, it would be helpful to offer some specific experience with personal space. Invite the children to stand inside a plastic hoop or on a carpet square or poly spot. Ask them to imagine they're inside a giant bubble, and suggest that they "paint" the inside of their bubble in any color they want. As the children pretend to paint, depending on what you see, you may pose questions such as the following:

- "What's usually the shape of a bubble?" (This will guide the children to think in terms of curving lines.)
- "How high does your bubble reach?"
- "Does your bubble go all the way underneath you?"
- "Does your bubble go all the way around you?"

Later, to help children understand that they carry their personal space with them through the space they share with others, you can play Shrinking Room.

Ask each child to step inside a hoop, pick it up, and put it around their waist. Then ask them to imagine that being inside the hoop is like being inside a giant bubble, or like being in a car on a highway (whichever image you think will work best with your group). Invite the children to move around the area without touching anyone else's bubble or car.

In the meantime, stand with your arms out to your sides, as far from the children as possible, and act as a "wall," beyond which they're not allowed to pass. Gradually, begin reducing the size of the area in which the children are allowed to move. Be sure to stop while the children are still able to move around without touching anyone else's hoop!

Note: If you don't have hoops, the children can still play this game by extending their arms to their sides. In this case, instead of avoiding contact with other hoops, they'll be avoiding contact with other hands.

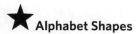
Alphabet Shapes

Learning Goal: Focus on letter shapes.

To familiarize children with letter shapes in a way that's much more fun than trying to copy letters on a worksheet multiple times, post the alphabet where the children can see it. Then call out a letter, and invite the children to create its shape with their body or body parts. Chances are their letters won't look anything like what you've posted, but that's okay. The purpose of the game is to help children consider the straight and curving lines that make up the letters, as well as the way these lines connect to one another.

Later, when the children have enough experience with cooperation, you can divide them into pairs or groups of three, who will work together to create letters.

 **Musical Magical Hoops**

Learning Goal: Focus on memory, color recognition, and listening skills.

This game combines elements of Musical Chairs and Statues but also tests the children's memory. Additionally, it promotes color recognition (art) and listening skills (emergent literacy).

You'll need a piece of recorded music, as well as several plastic hoops, in three colors, scattered around the floor or outside space. Explain that each hoop means moving in a different way. For example, if you have hoops in red, blue, and yellow laid out, the red could indicate marching, the blue might indicate shaking body parts, and the yellow stretching. These will be the only skills allowed inside the hoops.

While the music is playing, the children move in any way they want throughout the area. When the music stops (you pause it), they step into the closest hoop. For as long as the music is stopped, while inside the hoop, they perform the designated motor skill in any way they want.

 **It Takes Two**

Learning Goal: Focus on identifying body parts, cooperation, and solving problems.

This game requires an ability to identify body parts (science), to cooperate (social studies), and to solve problems. Your role in the game is to invite the children to connect pairs of body parts (matching parts, like right hands, left elbows, or right feet, or nonmatching parts, such as a hand and an elbow, an elbow and a shoulder, or a wrist and a hip, all of which you designate). With each connection, the children have two goals: to stay connected and to see how many ways they can move while connected. That means plenty of opportunity for experimentation and self-expression.

 **Simon Says**

Learning Goal: Focus on active listening and identifying body parts.

Played in the traditional way, the popular Simon Says is an elimination game and, therefore, not developmentally appropriate for young children. Typically, the children who most need practice with listening skills and body-part identification are the first to be eliminated. That makes little sense when we know children require such practice, but that doesn't mean we must throw out the game. It's wonderful for promoting listening skills (which fall under the heading of emergent literacy) and body-part identification (science). So, we make a slight change to the game's organization: Instead of one big group, the children gather in two circles or lines. Then, should children move without Simon's "permission," they transfer to the other circle or line. In this way the children have the chance to continue practicing and improving.

RECOMMENDED RESOURCES

You won't find many books devoted exclusively to guided play, but one possibility is *Serious Fun: How Guided Play Extends Children's Learning* by Marie Masterson and Holly Bohart.

I've written *Active Learning Across the Curriculum: Teaching the Way They Learn*. It's organized by content area and although not every activity fits the description of guided play, there are still many to choose from.

There is also a recorded webinar titled "Enhancing Knowledge and Skill Development by Gently Guiding Play." The webinar is presented by psychology expert and educator Kathy Hirsh-Pasek and NAEYC policy analyst Shana Cook (https://www.youtube.com/watch?v=xvMV1gf_Ibk).

PARTNERING WITH PARENTS

A survey by researchers at Temple University and the LEGO Foundation (Mader, 2023) found that most parents support play as a learning tool but are less certain about how to use it. Although research shows guided play leads to more learning, most parents surveyed believed their children learn more from free play.

Rather than share research articles on the benefits of guided play, you might simply let parents know that while free play has great value, if there are learning goals in mind, guided play is the way to go. The most important thing to explain to parents is that they may initiate an activity, but their child is free to take part in it in any way they choose. And any guidance a parent wants to offer must be *subtle* (e.g., a guiding question or comment as opposed to instruction).

In your communications with parents, you can share those games and activities from this chapter that lend themselves to a home environment. But in an interview with Mader (2023), Charlotte Anne Wright, one of the researchers in the study mentioned, pointed out that guided play at home doesn't have to look like it would in a classroom.

Wright uses the example of a walk through a park that sparks an exploration of shadows or different types of leaves or rocks. She suggests that a ride on a bus could be the inspiration for creating a story about what was seen. A trip to the laundromat could end with a sock-matching game. She says, "The goal is that it doesn't feel like something extra that requires special skills, but [it's] a way to change the lens on how we view everyday experiences and share with children to enrich them a little bit more."

CHAPTER 3

Big Body Play

The children can't even walk a block without becoming exhausted.
　　The children can't hold themselves upright these days. They're either slumping over their desks or leaning against something.
　　The children are falling out of their chairs!

　　I wish I could say these are unusual occurrences, but I can't. These are among the stories I hear from teachers everywhere, over and over again.
　　Then there are the news accounts and research studies reporting that since 2010, the rates of childhood obesity have continued to rise (Bailey, 2023), with the body mass index (BMI) nearly doubling in children ages 2 to 19 during the pandemic (Wang & Gago, 2024). To me, these trends are not just cause for concern—they're cause for panic.
　　The human body was built to *move*, especially in early childhood. If you've ever watched children run when they could walk, it's clear that the little ones were given both the ability and the impulse to move—a lot. All that movement is essential for physical development, strengthening bones and muscles and promoting the maturity of physical skills. But movement in early childhood is also essential to brain development, as it helps the brain form and connect neural pathways necessary for understanding, memory, and other cognitive skills. (See "Why Big Body Play?" later in the text for more reasons movement is essential in early childhood.)
　　Sadly, children are doing so little moving these days that their physical and cognitive development are being negatively impacted. When even the exertion of sitting upright has become too much for some of them, it's past time for concern.

WHY AREN'T CHILDREN MOVING?

For most children, gone are the days of playing tag, leaping from high places, rolling down hills, and running back up them—just because they could. Instead, most have become sedentary creatures with underdeveloped physical skills and adults in their lives who don't seem to realize the need for movement. SHAPE America, the Society of Health and Physical Educators, recommends that preschoolers engage in at least 60 minutes—and up to several hours—of physical activity *daily*. The American Heart Association recommends that children ages 3 to 5 be physically active throughout the day, with children ages 6 to 17 getting at least 60 minutes a day of moderate- to vigorous-intensity, mostly aerobic, physical activity per day.

Personally, I don't know a single child meeting any of those recommendations. Yes, I know that in these times such recommendations may seem impossible to achieve, but that doesn't mean we shouldn't try! At least in the trying we can get a bit closer to what's best for our children.

As mentioned in the book's introduction, there are several factors behind these phenomena. Among them are a focus on early academics and overscheduling, both of which have led to less time to—and less respect for—play. Then there's the fear of letting children out of sight and having them get hurt. These dynamics have had the greatest negative impact on big body play specifically. That's because big body play, sometimes called *large* or *gross motor* play, as the names imply, requires *space*. It involves large muscles (the trunk, along with legs and arms) and large movements, and is usually energetic and often noisy. The outdoors, then, is typically the best place for it. But few children have the access to the outdoors that their predecessors had.

Even when they do have access to outdoor play while in school or care, overly protective safety guidelines, worry about liability issues, and the tendency to want to bubble wrap children means the little ones aren't climbing trees and slides, swinging from monkey bars, or running with wild abandon.

Cartwheels, playing tag, and even running itself have been banned from far too many school playgrounds (even one would be too many) (Vines, 2012). Every time I read an article about another restriction placed on big body play (ExRx.net, n.d.), I'm frustrated that adults are prioritizing the avoidance of lawsuits and imagined fears over the real ones (e.g., the reasons behind the childhood obesity crisis).

There are other factors to consider as well. Parents and teachers might believe motor skills are important, but neither group feels it's their responsibility to promote their development. That may be because they assume motor-skill development happens without intervention—and I get that. We see babies roll over and begin to crawl and creep on their own, so it's easy to assume that children automatically acquire motor skills as their bodies develop. But maturation only means they'll be able to execute most movement skills at an immature or imperfect level. While we shouldn't expect mastery in early childhood, we do want to help children refine their movement skills and expand their movement vocabularies. Children who feel comfortable with their movement skills are more likely to keep moving, and that translates into a greater chance for lifelong health.

WHY BIG BODY PLAY?

I've written an entire textbook on movement (Pica, 2013), so it is challenging to answer this question in one section of one chapter. In short, big body play

- burns calories;
- contributes to bone density and strength (bones aren't fully developed until kids are in their teens and require weight-bearing activities to strengthen);
- promotes the five health-related fitness factors: muscular strength, muscular endurance, cardiovascular endurance, flexibility, and body composition; and
- stimulates growth of the heart, lungs, and other vital organs.

Big body play is the foremost kind of play needed to combat such issues as obesity, lethargy, and poor physical condition. The reason children are exhausted after walking a block is related to issues with all five of the health-related fitness factors. It's not unusual for adults with sedentary lifestyles to become exhausted while being physically active, but it's extremely unusual for children. Once, as I huffed and puffed my way up a big grassy hill, I watched young children *run* up that same hill with ease! (Sadly, one of the moms called out, "Don't run!" I bit my tongue to keep from saying something, but perhaps I shouldn't have.)

The reason many children have poor posture these days is because they have weak core and upper body strength. After all, how many activities do you see them participating in that engage the core (the central part of the body) and the upper torso? The problem begins when the children are infants and aren't given enough tummy time to strengthen their arms, shoulders, chest, and back muscles. It continues as they mature and are prohibited from hanging, swinging, and climbing.

And speaking of hanging and swinging, these are among the activities meant to help develop the proprioceptive and vestibular senses. Proprioception is awareness of the location of one's body and body parts in relation to the environment. With a properly developed proprioceptive sense, individuals can feed themselves without having to watch the fork approach their mouth, or climb stairs without looking at their feet. The vestibular sense detects motion and gravity and coordinates with the other senses to create an internal sense of balance. It also contributes to better visual tracking and self-regulation. When children have well-developed vestibular and proprioceptive senses, they can sit upright and stay that way. Without these senses, you get stories about children falling out of their chairs.

Pediatric occupational therapist Angela Hanscom tells us children should experience rapid vestibular input *daily*. That means "they need to go upside down, spin in circles, and roll down hills. They need authentic play experiences that get them moving in all different directions in order to stimulate the little hair cells found in the vestibular complex (located in the inner ear)" (Strauss, 2014).

Early childhood fitness expert Preston Blackburn offers another perspective. She writes

> When children don't push, pull, jump, or climb, they do not put pressure on their joints. This limited physical experience thwarts the development of the proprioceptive system and restricts their understanding of force, leading kids to use too much force (hitting instead of tagging), or too little (tapping instead of pressing). Without enough movement to develop the proprioceptive system, children's brains will search out this stimulus in other less productive ways: slamming into walls and floor, excessive roughhousing, and pushing heavy things over. These actions may look like bad behavior, poor self-regulation, or a lack of self-control. But, more likely, children demonstrating these behaviors are desperately seeking essential information about the body and how to use it. Movement is the only source of that critical information. (Blackburn, 2023)

As I've said, the human body was made to *move* and to grow and develop through movement. Unfortunately, at school or in many early learning environments, the functions of the brain tend to be valued over the functions of the body, which means it's too easy for the physical domain to be overlooked. But what if big body play also improves the functions of the brain? In fact, it does!

I'll give you just one important example of why the brain requires big body play: Moderate- to vigorous-intensity physical activity (which increases the breathing and heartbeat a little to a lot, respectively) pumps water, oxygen, and glucose to the brain. This is *brain food* that optimizes the brain's performance. As I often say, we would never consider leaving children's bodies unfed. We know the body requires the nutrients it gets from food. But when we prevent children from participating in active, big body play, we're depriving their brains of necessary nutrients.

Perhaps it shouldn't be surprising that a study of 4- and 5-year-olds found that those who struggle with such basic physical skills as standing on one foot, or even crawling, are much more likely to fall behind academically (Clark, 2012).

PUTTING THEORY INTO PRACTICE

I understand that most early childhood professionals haven't studied motor development. I've watched the royalties on my movement textbook dwindle as fewer and fewer teacher-prep programs include any courses on movement. But I want to assure you that a degree in motor development or physical education is *not* necessary to promote big body play with young children. I ask only that you provide time, space, and encouragement for gross motor movement, and that you apply the same level of observation to the children's physical development as you do to their cognitive and social-emotional development.

It's simple enough to make big body play part of your children's experience. In addition to time, space, and encouragement, you can be sure there are frequent opportunities for the children to experience locomotor, nonlocomotor, and other body-management skills.

Locomotor, or traveling, skills are all weight-bearing activities and, therefore, fall under the heading of "big body play." These skills include

- Crawling (on the belly)
- Creeping (on hands and knees)
- Walking
- Running
- Jumping (two-footed takeoff and landing)
- Leaping
- Galloping
- Hopping (landing on one foot)
- Sliding (a sideward gallop)
- Skipping (a combination of a step and a hop, with an uneven rhythm, that children often don't acquire until 6-and-a-half)

Children naturally engage in these gross motor skills, but you can inspire additional engagement with certain props and pieces of equipment. An obstacle course that includes a tunnel, large box, or a rope strung a foot above the ground offers practice with crawling and creeping. To inspire jumping *off*, you can make a low balance beam available, as well as log stumps or sturdy plastic crates of varying heights. A low balance beam also invites children to jump *over* or to leap. Child-sized instruments are likely to inspire marching (an exaggerated walk) and stick horses to inspire galloping.

Parachute play involves the nonlocomotor skills of bending and stretching, which activate the core and upper torso, as does "painting" the outside of the building with a paintbrush and bucket of water. And, of course, the right playground equipment will encourage such skills as climbing, hanging, and swinging, also necessary for core and upper body strength.

Following are some specific activity suggestions.

 Touch It

With the children scattered about the outside area, call out "Touch red!" The children then run to touch something red, whether it's an object or on someone else's clothing. They then run back to their original spots. Continue with as many colors as you can see.

You can also play this game with shapes ("Touch something round!"), textures (smooth, rough, hard, soft, etc.), or objects ("Touch a tree trunk!" "Touch a blade of grass!" "Touch a wall!)" To make the activity more aerobic, call out the next challenge as soon as the children have returned to their original spots.

Blob Tag

Tag games that eliminate can result in too much waiting-around time. Blob Tag, on the other hand, keeps the children moving.

Choose one child to be It. Everybody tagged also becomes It. The result is a cluster of children that keeps growing until there's just one big "blob" running around together. The last person tagged is the first person to be It in the next round.

Bubble Chase

Nothing could be simpler than blowing bubbles for the children to try to catch, inspiring both running and jumping.

Rabbits and 'Roos

Talk to the children about rabbits and kangaroos, and ask about such features as size and weight. Then invite the children to alternate between moving like rabbits and kangaroos. Which do they think would jump the most heavily? Because size and weight are math concepts—as are such quantitative concepts as high, low, light, and heavy, this qualifies as a math experience.

"Pop Goes the Weasel"

Play, sing, or hum "Pop Goes the Weasel," inviting the children to walk along until they hear the "pop." At the sound of the "pop," they jump into the air and then continue walking.

Once the children have become accustomed to this, make the activity more challenging by inviting them to jump *and* change direction each time they hear the "pop." This activity falls under the content areas of music, emergent literacy (active listening), and social studies (self-regulation).

 **Hopscotch**

Jumping and hopping are both part of this popular game. The number recognition involved falls under the content area of math.

 **Hoop Jump**

You'll need one plastic hoop per child for this activity. Arrange them in a circle, and place them close enough so they're touching. Each child stands inside a hoop. At your signal, the children begin jumping around the circle, from inside one hoop to inside the next.

When the children are adept at jumping from hoop to hoop, invite them to try leaping (one leg extended to the front and the other to the back) from hoop to hoop. Finally, when they have enough balance to be successful at it, challenge them to hop from hoop to hoop.

RECOMMENDED RESOURCES

- I'm a big believer in not reinventing the wheel. So, if you're looking for movement activities, complete with original music, I'd like to recommend my Moving & Learning Series. It includes *Toddlers Moving & Learning, Preschoolers & Kindergartners Moving & Learning*, and *Early Elementary Children Moving & Learning*.
- Another resource is Frances Carlson's *Big Body Play: Why Boisterous, Vigorous, and Very Physical Play Is Essential to Children's Development and Learning*. You'll find a webinar on the topic here: https://www.earlychildhoodwebinars.com/webinars/big-body-play-something-scary-good-children-frances-carlson/.
- If the connection between movement and the brain interests you, I recommend Dr. John Ratey's *Spark: The Revolutionary New Science of Exercise and the Brain* or Carla Hannaford's *Smart Moves: Why Learning Is Not All in Your Head*.
- SHAPE America's physical-activity guidelines for infants, toddlers, and preschoolers are outlined here: https://www.shapeamerica.org/MemberPortal/standards/guidelines/activestart.aspx.

PARTNERING WITH PARENTS

I dislike having to justify movement in children's lives, but I'll do whatever it takes to convince parents that their kids need it! Given that, and the fact that today's parents are so concerned about academic success, I suggest you share information related to physical activity's contribution to the brain and cognitive performance.

You can include information and research from this chapter, Sahlberg and Doyle's book, *Let the Children Play*, or Dr. Ratey's book in your communications with parents. If you send emails or newsletters, you can also include the link to a particularly interesting article or print the article and place it in the children's cubbies or folders. (Possible articles include "The Importance of Movement for Children" [https://www.playstreet.in/2021/10/21/the-importance-of-movement-for-children/] and "How Do We Build Successful Kids?: Play Hard. Move Lots. Learn More" [https://www.communityplaythings.com/resources/articles/building-successful-kids].) Either way, you might want to include a note expressing your excitement about finding the piece and sharing it with parents. I know a lot of early childhood professionals are concerned about coming across as more knowledgeable than parents, but your enthusiasm should prevent that.

Of course, you should also encourage movement for movement's sake. Parents want their children to be strong and healthy, so they should know the reasons why big body play is essential from a physical-development perspective as well.

Suggest ways in which it's still possible to get kids moving year-round. How about after-dinner walks, trips to the playground, and physical family outings, like hiking or roller skating (as opposed to such sedentary activities as watching TV or going to the movies)? Families can take advantage of seasonal events in their area. Are there pumpkin festivals in the fall? Sledding parties in the winter? Summer fairs or carnivals? Places for strawberry, blueberry, or apple picking?

Finally, you might also recommend toys that encourage physical activity, as opposed to those leading to sedentary behaviors. Examples of the former include bikes and trikes, scooters, skates, balls of various sizes, and plastic hoops.

CHAPTER 4

Outdoor Play

Despite its many benefits, today's children spend far less time playing outdoors than their predecessors did. On the home front, according to a 2018 study, children ages 3 to 12 are spending 35% less time playing outside than their parents did (Business Wire, 2018). A United Kingdom study (Kennedy, 2018) found that children are spending only half the time playing outside as did their parents. A 2015 study from Michigan State University determined that children ages 6 to 17 spend only 7 minutes a day in unstructured outdoor play (Hintzen, 2015)! Although that study is almost a decade old, there's every indication the situation has not improved since then.

In public schools, according to the American Association for the Child's Right to Play (n.d.), about 40% of U.S. schools have eliminated recess, and some elementary schools have been built without playgrounds! In those schools that still offer recess, most children can expect to have far less recess time than I did as a child in public school. Then, two recesses a day, each for 30 minutes, was the norm. Currently, two per day is almost unheard of, with many schools providing less than half an hour for the single recess they do offer. One mom wrote to me because she was fighting against the decision of her kindergartner's school to offer only *one 10-minute recess*. Over the course of just a few weeks in school, her daughter had changed from a happy child to one who was stressed and displaying challenging behaviors.

Sadly, even in private early learning and childcare programs, it's not unusual for children to spend less time playing outside than did earlier cohorts. There are a variety of reasons for these changes. On the home front, overscheduling is a primary factor. American children between 3 and 12 participate in an average of five structured activities a week (Business Wire, 2018). Many preschoolers also are now given homework (Korbey, 2012), leaving little time for outdoor play, which many parents may not consider a priority.

Fear is another major factor keeping children indoors. One teacher told me her daughter was outdoors almost all the time as a child (as were all children of my generation) but that her grandchildren are rarely allowed outside. A mom told me her 6-year-old son wasn't allowed to play outside by himself. When I asked why not, she replied, "Because you never know who might be lurking around the corner."

Fear, unfortunately, has become a driving factor in childhood today. Where once the local and national news aired only at 6 and 11 p.m., sharing time with both weather and sports on the few available television stations, we now have access to news in a variety of formats 24 hours a day. (I'm old enough to remember when all TV stations shut down for the night at 11:30!) And much of what is promoted during those 24 hours is fear.

Fear certainly was evident in a Facebook discussion about the appropriate age to allow a child to walk to school alone. (While there are no federal guidelines on this, many states leave it to parents to decide, with others recommending ages 8 to 12 as a minimum. The American Academy of Pediatrics suggests children are ready at age 10.) One mom replied she'd allowed it when her child was 15 but only because she was watching from a hill. Another mom contended it wasn't safe to leave a child alone *ever*. I tried to convince them it's the safest time to be a kid in America (Ingraham, 2015)—and that even the National Center for Missing and Exploited Children contends there's no such thing as stranger danger (Covel, 2023)—but it was a futile effort.

Of course, even with free time and parents who allow children to go outside, the competition for children's attention is tough these days. Many children have more access to screen time than to outdoor time and, therefore, prefer the former. I'll never forget the story Richard Louv told in *Last Child in the Woods* (2005). He'd asked a 4th-grader if he preferred the indoors or the outdoors. "The indoors," the child said, because that's where the electrical outlets are.

In public schools, the reason most often cited for the elimination of recess is more "instructional time," the idea being that more time spent at desks will improve grades and test scores. But that patently ignores what we now know about how the brain learns best, and any decision-maker with a working knowledge of the research would realize how counterproductive this is.

It's also counterproductive when children in private preschools and childcare programs spend considerably more time indoors than outdoors. Often, this is a result of the "earlier-is-better" myth, which causes paying parents to prioritize academics over playtime. The curriculum pushdown in kindergarten and beyond also means there are unrealistic demands preschool children must meet to be "ready" for kindergarten in ways they previously weren't. This places enormous pressure on early childhood professionals and leaves far less time for outdoor play than young children should have.

WHY OUTDOOR PLAY?

In this section, I'll address outdoor play in general, separate from recess, which many early childhood educators see as related to public schooling only.

Let's start with the physical benefits of being outside. As I commented in the previous chapter, the best place for big body play is typically outdoors. Here children can run and jump and engage in activities often considered too large and loud for indoors. As they do so, they're practicing and refining emerging physical skills—necessary if they're to become physically active and fit individuals. Active outdoor play not only burns calories, it also promotes cardiovascular endurance, muscular strength, muscular endurance, flexibility, and body composition. Again, these are the five health-related factors that determine a child's physical fitness.

Then there's the production of vitamin D, which is aided by natural light. This vitamin is needed for healthy bones, muscles, joints, and tissues. The outside light also improves sleep patterns, increases productivity, and makes us feel happier. These would be reasons enough to go outside!

But there is one more physical reason, and it's a recent phenomenon resulting both from too much screen time and too little time spent outdoors. In the past few years, there has been an increase in myopia diagnoses (Jargon, 2023), to the point that it is being called an epidemic. Myopia, or nearsightedness, develops in children, beginning at age 5, and is closely related to lack of exposure to outdoor light.

Nearsightedness may not seem to be a major problem, but glasses and doctors' appointments are expensive. Also, if left untreated, it could lead to further problems, including glaucoma, cataracts, retinal detachment, and even blindness (Jargon, 2023). A study published in the *British Journal of Ophthalmology* (Lingham et al., 2020) concluded that exposure to the brighter light of the outdoors can indeed reduce the risk of myopia.

For those whose priority is learning, I would point out that studies have shown children who play outdoors have greater problem-solving and creative abilities (Hamilton, 2014). Outside, children are more likely to invent games and activities. As they do, they're able to express themselves and learn about the world in their own way. They feel safe and in control, which promotes autonomy, decision-making, and organizational skills. Creating rules for games (as young children like to do) promotes an understanding of why rules are necessary. Although the children are just playing to have fun, they learn

- communication skills, as they invent, modify, and enforce the rules;
- math skills, as they count, compare, and observe such quantitative concepts as big and small and first and last; and
- social skills, as they learn to collaborate and cooperate.

All of this helps advance physical, social-emotional, and cognitive development—that is, the development of the whole child. Additionally, time spent outside helps children come to value the outdoors. This is significant because it's unlikely that children who spend most of their time indoors will learn to care for the environment.

WHY RECESS?

In Finland, schoolchildren receive a 15-minute recess after every 45 minutes of instruction. Why? Because their "world-renowned childhood education system [is] based on a strong foundation of learning through play, [and is] a system that [provides] for constant bursts of play and playful discovery in school all the way up to high school . . ." (Sahlberg and Doyle, 2019, p. 16).

In Finland, policymakers have based their education system on the research. For example, research shows that children (and adults) produce more when they have breaks than they do without them. That's because, in part, the human brain can consume only so much information at a time (Jensen, 2000). Also, Dr. Robert Murray, a pediatrician and coauthor of an AAP statement on the importance of recess, wrote, "Children need to have downtime between complex cognitive challenges. . . . They tend to be less able to process information the longer they are held to a task" (Rochman, 2012). This was validated by the research of Karrie Godwin and her colleagues, which determined that attention improved when children received their lessons in shorter periods (Godwin et al., 2016).

All this research—and there is a lot of it—points to the fact that more "instructional time" clearly is counterintuitive. And the argument that there's no time for recess simply doesn't fly. Researchers Olga Jarrett and Darlene Maxwell determined that children were more on-task and less fidgety on days when they had recess. A 15-minute recess, in fact, translated into 20 minutes more on-task time (Jarrett & Maxwell, 2000).

Based on her extensive study, science writer Annie Murphy Paul (2021) maintains, "Parents, teachers, and administrators who want students to achieve academically should be advocating for an increase in physically active recess time" (p. 51).

But academic achievement isn't the only reason children need recess. There are all the benefits of time spent outdoors, cited in the last section. Additionally, recess is one of the last bastions of unstructured play, which reduces stress in children (Clay, 2023). Since today's children have ample occasion to feel stress, we should be looking to any natural—and simple—means of relieving it.

And we can't forget social development. Children need to learn to be social creatures. Recess may be the only time during the day when children have an opportunity to experience socialization and real communication. Typically, while in school, children are not allowed to interact during class, when lining up, or when moving from one area of the school to another.

Some school policies even prevent children from talking to one another during lunch. And because neighborhoods are not what they used to be, once the school day ends, there may be little chance for social interaction. How can children with so few opportunities to socialize and communicate be expected to live and work together as adults? When and where will they have learned how?

Pasi Sahlberg and William Doyle (2019), authors of *Let the Children Play: How More Play Will Save Our Schools and Help Children Thrive*, offer strong words regarding the elimination of recess. They call it "a spectacle of cruelty to American children, a real-life, flesh-and-blood, slow-motion horror movie affecting millions of girls and boys over the years" (p. 117).

Decision-makers who implement no-recess policies might want to consider how they would feel if forced to work all day, every day with *no breaks*. Or, I would add, if decisions were being made for them without the necessary and appropriate information.

PUTTING THEORY INTO PRACTICE

The outdoor area is where children are best able to practice and refine such gross motor skills as running, leaping, and galloping. However, it's also the perfect area for the practice of manipulative skills (those in which an object is manipulated) and body-management skills. For instance, it's conducive to the performance of such ball-handling skills as throwing, catching, and striking. Also, children have opportunities to perform such actions as pushing a swing, pulling a wagon, and lifting and carrying movable objects. Body-management skills include climbing, hanging, swinging, and balancing, all of which can be experienced on outdoor equipment.

Following are some other opportunities presented in the outdoors:

- Rolling, necessary for the development of the proprioceptive and vestibular senses (see Chapter 3), is more likely to occur on grass than on a classroom floor.
- Riding tricycles, virtually impossible indoors, contributes to muscular strength and endurance.
- Parachute games, which offer a number of benefits, including upper torso exercise and the development of flexibility, require a large, open area that may not be available in the classroom.
- Blowing bubbles for the children to chase and catch should be enjoyed outside if the game is to be successful in promoting cardiovascular endurance and muscular strength and endurance.

However, it's important to remember that many games and activities played indoors can also be played outdoors. Simply by bringing them outside, you're allowing for more possibilities and a change in perspective for the children. Playing Follow the Leader outdoors, for example, likely offers more options for pathways and changes in direction, as the children maneuver around trees and equipment. Obstacle courses created outside allow for the inclusion of natural materials, providing the children with a variety of sensory experiences. Thanks to the invention of the smartphone, even musical games can easily be transferred outdoors. If the children have more space in which to play Statues, for example, that's likely to result in even more—and perhaps a greater variety of—movement. And a treasure hunt is always a popular activity, whether played indoors or outdoors. But the latter offers more sensory experiences and, of course, more space in which to roam and discover.

I want to emphasize that it is *critical* that educators never withhold recess or outdoor time as punishment. Spending time outside is a right for children and not a privilege to be granted or denied. Furthermore, not only is the denial of recess almost never a logical consequence for any perceived infraction but it doesn't work to deter the behaviors that typically deny children recess. If it did, there wouldn't be so much anecdotal evidence indicating that the same children have recess withheld from them over and over again.

Here are some specific outdoor activity ideas.

A Listening Walk

Rather than simply going for a walk with the children, take a listening walk, making it a more interesting experience. Explain that as they walk the children are going to listen either for manmade sounds or sounds in nature (your choice, or you can allow the children to choose). Examples of the former would include the children's footsteps, a car horn, a truck engine, or a train whistle. Sounds in nature might include a cat's meow, a dog's bark, the wind rustling leaves, or birds singing. Once you return from the walk, you can add more movement to the experience by inviting the children to physically demonstrate the sources of some of the sounds heard. The active listening involved in this activity falls under the content area of emergent literacy.

Shadow Tag

You'll need a sunny day for this game. Designate one player to be It. This player's assignment is to tag other players by stepping on their shadows. When children are tagged this way, they are frozen until another player steps on their shadows and frees them.

⭐ Bottle Bowling

Typically, bowling requires great eye-hand coordination and a lot of waiting. But young children aren't particularly adept at either (eye-hand coordination isn't fully developed until 9 or 10 years old, and we know how they feel about waiting). That's why this game involves larger objects than the standard bowling ball and pins and is played in pairs.

You'll need two to three empty soda bottles per pair of children and one beach ball or large playground ball per pair. Arrange the soda bottles in close proximity for each pair of children and give each pair a ball. One child stands near the "pins" while the other bowls—that is, rolls the ball and tries to knock the bottles down. The second child then retrieves the ball while the first resets the pins. Then the second child takes a turn bowling. The children continue in this manner, taking turns for as long as they stay interested.

⭐ Ring Toss

This game requires one large, empty soda bottle or plastic cone and one plastic hoop per child. Line up the soda bottles or plastic cones side by side and spaced far enough apart so plastic hoops placed over them don't interfere with each other. Line the children up similarly, each opposite a bottle or cone (and only a short distance away) and give each child a hoop. Encourage the children to try to toss their hoop over the cone or bottle opposite them. After every unsuccessful try, they simply retrieve the hoop and try again. With each successful try, they can take a step further away from the cone, or bottle if they desire.

⭐ Creatures in the Clouds

There are no rules for Creatures in the Clouds, nor should there be. On a day that's partly cloudy, you can either invite children to lie on their backs and try to find animals or objects in the clouds, or you can point out a creature you've found yourself, and let the children decide whether or not they also want to look. This should be an activity that offers the children downtime and an opportunity to set their imaginations free. In other words, this is a time that allows you to step back. There is no scaffolding required here!

RECOMMENDED RESOURCES

- You can listen to an 11-minute podcast titled "Why Recess Matters and How to Defend It" here: https://www.bamradionetwork.com/track/why-recess-matters-how-to-defend-it/. Gail Connelly, former executive director of the National Association of Elementary School Principals, is the guest.
- If you're going to advocate for the children's right to outdoor time and recess, IPA/USA (https://ipausa.org)—or its international version (https://ipaworld.org)—has a great deal of information you can use, as do the following two resources.
- The goal of LiiNK (https://liinkproject.tcu.edu) is to improve brain development through physical activity and outdoor exposure every day.
- Global Recess Alliance (https://globalrecessalliance.org) is made up of scholars, health, and education leaders who speak publicly about the essential nature of recess for all children.
- You'll find several research articles on recess here: https://onlinelibrary.wiley.com/toc/17461561/2022/92/10.
- Free-Range Kids (https://www.freerangekids.com) is the place to go to learn "How Parents and Teachers Can Let Go and Let Grow." Their mission is "fighting the belief that our children are in constant danger from creeps, kidnapping, germs, grades, flashers, frustration, failure, baby snatchers, bugs, bullies, men, sleepovers and/or the perils of a non-organic grape." In other words, this is where you go when you want help debunking the myth that children are in greater peril than they've ever been. This movement began when founder Lenore Skenazy wrote *Free-Range Kids: How Parents and Teachers Can Let Go and Let Grow*.
- Save Our Schools (https://www.saveourschoolsmarch.org/legal-age-to-walk-home-from-school-alone-usa/) offers considerations for parents making a decision about when their child can walk to school, as well as safety steps to take.

> ### PARTNERING WITH PARENTS
>
> We know that parents want the best for their children, which includes wanting their children to be healthy and to do well in school. So, don't be shy about sharing the many benefits of the outdoors with them in whatever ways you can.
>
> Many parents, like many adults in general, don't know the research about the importance of breaks. As a result, they may agree with decision-makers who want to keep kids at their desks for as long as possible. And they may not understand that the absence of breaks is the cause behind

the unraveling they witness when their little ones come home from school. Indeed, many parents, who experienced sufficient recess and outdoor time when young, don't realize their children aren't receiving the same. It's only when they question the exhaustion and stress visible in their children that they discover this is happening.

If they should discover it, they'll likely turn to you first. If your administrator or school district is responsible for the lack of outdoor time, I recommend you share this information with parents and recruit them to your cause! There's strength in numbers, and if teachers and parents work together to restore outdoor time or recess, there is a greater chance of success.

I suspect you'll have less success trying to convince parents their children aren't in constant danger. So, it might be best to let others do it for you. One possibility is sharing the Ingraham piece in *The Washington Post*, cited in the references. You might also use *Free-Range Kids* as part of a book study among teachers and parents.

Share the International Myopia Institute's recommendation that children spend 80 to 120 minutes per day in the outdoor light. And let parents know that this doesn't have to happen all at once; shorter periods add up. They should also know that children are more likely to be interested in the outdoors if their parents are.

To help parents recall the joys of a childhood spent outside, many of my colleagues employ the brilliant strategy of *asking* them to remember. At a teacher-parent gathering, for example, you can ask parents—either individually or as a group—what they most enjoyed about their childhood. *Many* of them will recall time spent outdoors playing. And if you ask them what their favorite thing in elementary school was, many of them will reply, "Recess!" If we can help them remember how good it felt to be playing outside—and/or the freedom and joy of recess—perhaps they'll realize they want that for their children too.

CHAPTER 5

Nature Play

You may be curious as to why nature play has a chapter separate from outdoor play. Simply put, outdoor play doesn't necessarily involve nature. Nature play always does.

Janet Dyment is an associate professor in the School of Education at the University of Tasmania. She describes nature play as ". . . play activities in outdoor settings where natural elements feature, such as logs, rocks and water, as opposed to conventional manufactured play equipment" (quoted in First Five Years, 2020). Nature play can occur anywhere there are natural elements: at a park, at the beach, in the woods, and in a backyard. And it can occur in the outdoor space of an early learning program.

Some adults may question why children would want to play with objects like sticks and stones when there are modern playground structures, toy trucks, and trikes available. But young children have always been fascinated by the natural world, whether it's watching the progress of a caterpillar cross the grass, pouring sand from one container to another, or stomping in mud puddles. The natural world is a place of *wonder* for children, and wonder—that sense of curiosity and amazement—leads children to question, explore, and *discover*. Wonder leads to authentic learning and, it must be said, is more difficult to come by indoors or wherever children are engaging with single-use toys or digital devices requiring no imagination on the child's part.

Unfortunately, there are multiple forces preventing children from experiencing nature as their predecessors did. Among them are the fear factor, overscheduling, and competition from screens, all described in the last chapter. Further, there is the modern compulsion to keep children "safe"— the meaning of which has expanded to include preventing even bumps and bruises. All these factors have become greater priorities in our culture than exposure to nature.

Fortunately, the number of early childhood professionals aware of nature's benefits is growing, resulting in an increase in nature-based programs. You may not be able to offer a full-fledged outdoor learning program, but you can still ensure the children have opportunities to experience nature play.

WHY NATURE PLAY?

In *Last Child in the Woods*, author Richard Louv coined the term "nature-deficit disorder," which he contends "describes the human costs of alienation from nature, among them: diminished use of the senses, attention difficulties, and higher rates of physical and emotional illnesses" (2005, p. 34).

Let's address the sensory issue first. The outdoors is a virtual wonderland for the senses, through which young children acquire significant information. There are different and incredible things for the children to *see* (dandelions, clouds, and shadows), to *hear* (cicadas, birdsong, leaves rustling in the wind), to *smell* (flowers and the rain-soaked ground), to *touch* (a fuzzy caterpillar or the bark of a tree), and even to *taste* (newly fallen snow, a raindrop, or a freshly picked blueberry). In contrast, children who spend most of their time experiencing life through television, computers, and even books use a maximum of two senses (hearing and sight), and that can affect their perceptual abilities.

Pediatric occupational therapist Angela Hanscom (2016) tells us that nature enhances all the senses and cites studies backing her up. Among the examples she offers:

- The soft colors and subtle visual stimuli in nature "have a calming effect on a child's sensory system." (p. 99)
- Sounds in nature "provide a restorative effect" following stressful situations (p. 101). Listening to birds, in particular, offers many sensory benefits.
- Nature enhances the sense of touch. Hanscom says, "The sensations of getting dirty and messy in real mud offer children an invaluable rich and tactile experience . . . through exposure to various tactile experiences, children increase their tolerance to different touch sensations." (p. 103)
- Nature enhances the sense of taste and smell because it "provides a variety of taste and texture experiences that are hard to replicate in toys or other man-made items" (p. 107). Among the consequences of too few taste and texture experiences are a decreased tolerance for new foods and scents.

Additionally, the amazing sights, sounds, and textures that fill the natural world promote the development of aesthetics in young children. Aesthetic awareness refers to a heightened sensitivity to the beauty around us. It's something that can serve children well when, as adolescents and adults, the world seems less than beautiful. Indeed, Richard Louv (2005) contends that when we deny children nature, we deny them beauty. Witnessing a sunset, plucking a bright red apple from a tree and sinking teeth into its crisp juiciness, making angels in the snow, or lying in the grass are immediate, sensual experiences that enrich our lives in ways we simply can't measure.

When it comes to general health, there's plenty of indication that nature improves it. When children move in natural surroundings, they often move in different ways than if moving indoors. There are puddles to jump over, trees to avoid, and tree stumps to jump from. The uneven ground requires greater balance and strength. Children lift and carry those sticks and stones mentioned earlier. Also, there's generally more space in which to move outside. All of this increases the children's movement vocabulary and thus, their physical fitness.

Also, environment researcher Ming Kuo has determined that nature protects us from cardiovascular, respiratory, and musculoskeletal diseases, and more, primarily by boosting the immune system (Science Daily, 2015). She explains that exposure to nature puts the body into "rest and digest" mode—the opposite of "fight-or-flight" mode, which shuts down nonessential systems, including the immune system. She says, "When we are in nature in that relaxed state, and our body knows that it's safe, it invests resources toward the immune system."

Obviously, anything that puts us in a relaxed state is also good for mental health. The Mental Health Foundation (n.d.) tells us a connection to nature results in less depression and anxiety and played a critical role in our mental health during the pandemic. I, for one, am certain that spending time on my deck, observing the birds and changes in the trees during lockdown, was a lifesaver for me.

Scott Sampson (2016), author of *How to Raise a Wild Child,* contends that regular exposure to nature can help relieve mood disorders and attention deficits in children and can reduce bullying. For those concerned with academic achievement, Sampson further says that time in nature can even improve academic performance. It does so by reducing stress, which we know to be detrimental to learning, and by improving attention, boosting self-discipline, and increasing motivation (Kuo et al., 2019).

In terms of social-emotional development, the late Stephen R. Kellert, who was a professor of social ecology, had much to say about the "humanistic" value of nature, which stresses a strong emotional attachment to it. He wrote, "Bonding with elements of the natural world is viewed as instrumental in developing intimacy, companionship, trust, capacities for social relationship, and affiliation and in enhancing self-confidence and self-esteem through giving, receiving and sharing affection" (Kellert, 2002, p. 130). This, he said, contrasts with a "negativistic" value, which "reflects the avoidance, fear, and rejection of nature" (p. 131).

The authors of *The Great Outdoors: Advocating for Natural Spaces for Young Children* (Rivkin & Schein, 2014) tell us there's one very basic reason children need to experience being outside: humans evolved in the outdoors. They, thus, have a link with nature that can't be replaced and that can even be atrophied by technology.

Richard Louv (2005) wrote, "Parents, educators, other adults, institutions—the culture itself—may say one thing to children about nature's gifts, but so many of our actions and messages—especially the ones we cannot hear ourselves deliver—are different" (p. 14). When we keep children indoors, one regrettable message we convey is that nature is of little significance. How, then, are children to learn to care for the environment? Why would they work to preserve something they've been taught to disregard, or for which they have so little feeling? Considering our environment is the only one we have, it's to everyone's advantage if our children learn to love and value it when they're young, and that necessitates having firsthand experience of it.

Or, as George Eliot (2003) said, "We could never have loved the earth so well if we had had no childhood in it" (p. 45).

PUTTING THEORY INTO PRACTICE

If possible, I would recommend that children go barefoot when outside. Although many adults tend to view bare feet as problematic—often from a safety point of view—going barefoot can contribute much to children's experience of the natural world. Children have been moving in sneakers for physical activity for so long we seem to have forgotten that feet do have sentient qualities. In fact, they are the most nerve-rich parts of the human body. They can be used to grip the ground for strength and balance, and their different parts (toes, ball, sole, heel) can be more easily felt and used when bare.

Angela Hanscom (2016) tells us

> Walking outdoors offers natural messages to children's feet as they walk on different-sized pebbles and uneven ground. The resistance and inconsistency nature offers integrates reflexes in the foot and forms strong arches. Going barefoot out in nature helps to develop normal gait patterns, balance, and tolerance of touch in the feet, all of which provide a strong foundation for confident and fluid movement. (p. 107)

Young children feel a natural affinity for the ground, and that affinity can be enhanced by removing all barriers between it and the feet. Moreover, going barefoot can help the feet to develop naturally, as opposed to conforming to the shape of shoes.

Susan J. Oliver and Edgar Klugman (2005) offer recommendations for making the most of nature and outdoor play. Among them are the following:

- Educators should have a positive attitude about outdoor playtime, be ready and willing to work with the weather, children's interests, gender differences, and more—and should create a play climate that is flexible and supportive.
- Outdoor play time should be structured so children have sufficient time and facilitation to engage in complex, integrated, in-depth activities or explorations; can exercise their sense of curiosity and creativity; and can participate in a range of developmentally appropriate experiences.
- If the weather keeps you indoors too often . . . children may miss important experiential learning about rain or wind or snow. Work with their parents to provide outdoor clothing that offers the option of going outdoors nearly every day. (p. 7)

In terms of nature play itself, children will find all sorts of imaginative ways to use natural materials, from building forts to constructing towers to imagining them as other objects. A stick, for example, could become anything from a light saber to a flagpole. A dandelion might become part of a "meal," and a log become a balance beam, rocket ship, or ship at sea. Children can envision possibilities far beyond what we adults tend to imagine.

For the most part, when we talk about nature play, we're referring to free play. The children interact with natural materials in whatever ways they choose—responsibly and within limits, of course. But that doesn't mean you can't create additional possibilities by adding to the natural materials available. Possibilities include

- A sandbox
- A tub filled with water
- A mud pit (someplace where soil and water can be mixed together)
- Tree stumps
- Fallen logs
- Loose parts such as feathers and shells

Also, guided play isn't out of the question. Touch It, A Listening Walk, and Creatures in the Clouds, described in previous chapters, are examples. Here are more ideas for nature play.

Nature's Music

Invite the children to explore the possibilities for *sound* with natural materials. How does the sound of a stick differ from that of a rock? How many different sounds can they create with each item?

 **Going on a Treasure Hunt**

Children love a treasure hunt. Create a list of items for the children to find and collect, making sure that all items on the list are available in your environment. Possibilities include a smooth stone, a leaf, a pinecone, a blade of grass, and a twig.

 **Nature's Art**

Invite the children to create art with the natural materials they collect.

 Mix It Up

Add plastic cups, measuring cups, and spoons to the sandbox, tub of water, or mud pit to encourage new avenues of exploration.

RECOMMENDED RESOURCES

- You can watch the international, award-winning film, *Nature Play: Take Childhood Back*, here: https://www.natureplayfilm.com.
- For city dwellers, NAEYC offers an article titled "From Puddles to Pigeons: Learning About Nature in Cities." It can be found here: https://www.naeyc.org/resources/pubs/yc/nov2018/learning-about-nature-cities.
- The National Wildlife Foundation (https://www.nwf.org) offers subscriptions to *Ranger Rick*, as well as assistance in developing outdoor classrooms. And although they are no longer publishing guides for educators, there are dozens of past guides to peruse.
- If you're looking for resources and research, Children and Nature Network (https://www.childrenandnature.org) offers more than enough! They also have a Facebook group: https://www.facebook.com/childrenandnature/.
- You may need to promote the messy aspect of nature play. "Getting Adults on Board with Messy Nature Play" (https://www.newswise.com/articles/getting-adults-on-board-with-messy-nature-play) can help.

PARTNERING WITH PARENTS

- Some of the suggestions from the previous chapter—for example, alerting parents their children need 80 to 120 minutes per day in the outdoor light—are applicable here as well. And, of course, you'll want to share some of the research from this chapter with parents using whatever vehicles work best for you.
- If you're planning a book study with teachers and parents, I highly recommend Angela Hanscom's *Balanced and Barefoot* (2016). It makes the case for nature play in childhood in a conversational and accessible way and includes strategies parents can use to get their children engaged with nature.
- You might also choose to offer a viewing of *Nature Play*, the film mentioned earlier, for a parent-teacher night.
- If you've subscribed to *Ranger Rick* for your classroom, show it to parents—perhaps especially to those parents whose children have displayed the most enthusiasm for it—and recommend they subscribe to it at home.
- Child Mind Institute offers an article you can share with parents. It's titled "Ideas for Getting Your Kids Into Nature," and you can find it here: https://childmind.org/article/ideas-for-getting-your-kids-into-nature.

CHAPTER 6

Risky Play

Researcher and professor Ellen Beate Hansen Sandseter (2007) defines *risky play* as "a thrilling and exciting activity that involves a risk of physical injury, and play that provides opportunities for challenge, testing limits, exploring boundaries and learning about injury risk." Given that it involves the possibility of physical injury, it's not surprising that this type of play has become the most inaccessible to children today. Parental fear, as well as fear of litigation on the part of administrators and teachers, means children have fewer opportunities to take such "risks" as climbing trees, swinging from monkey bars, performing cartwheels, or even running on the playground. In this age of "bubble-wrapped" children, adults are afraid of bumps and bruises, but, also, even mistakes and other such perceived failures are considered undesirable for children to experience.

Many years ago, I moved next door to a family that included a 7-year-old boy, and over time I witnessed him sustain bumps, bruises, bloodied body parts, and even broken bones. Clarke fell while running. He fell while learning to skate. He fell out of trees. His parents picked him up and, if necessary, took him to the emergency room. While his parents naturally were upset to see their child hurt, there was no excessive drama. Clarke was experiencing a typical childhood. His bumps and bruises were a rite of passage.

Nowadays, such a childhood is atypical. As I recalled in Chapter 3, I once heard a mom shout at a child to stop running *uphill on grass*! I, on the other hand, had been marveling that the boy's cardiovascular endurance and muscular strength allowed him to run on a surface I struggled to ascend at a walking pace. "Don't run" is just one of many cautionary phrases with which today's children are far too familiar. Others include

- "Stop that!"
- "Not so high!"
- "Not so fast!"
- "No!"
- "Don't do that; you'll get hurt!"
- "Don't spin; you'll get dizzy!"
- "Get down!"

But I suspect the one phrase children likely hear most often is, "Be careful!"—especially if the children are girls. One study determined that parents cautioned their daughters—and were more likely to assist them—far more often than they did their sons, whom they encouraged to complete the physical task at hand (Morrongiello & Dawber, 1999). Another study concluded that parents warn their daughters to be careful *four times* more often than they do their sons (O'Neal et al., 2016). As a result, girls are less likely to try challenging physical tasks and are more likely to "avoid activities outside [their] comfort zone" (Paul, 2016).

However, outright cautions aren't the only ways in which children—both boys and girls—receive the message that risks are to be avoided at all costs. The following are just a few examples of the not-so-subliminal messages adults convey.

- When a school or early learning program removes all traditional playground equipment and replaces it with safe, sanitized plastic, children intuit the intention.
- When schools ban cartwheels during recess despite no previous cartwheel injuries, children learn that physical activity is hazardous (Skenazy, 2017).
- When cities ban sledding, children realize that such time-honored traditions are of less importance than staying "safe" (Fox, 2020).
- When in addition to banning cartwheels a school also disallows tag *and* replaces all balls with Nerf balls (Anderssen, 2013), the message is loud and clear: Play is risky, and risks are unacceptable. And apparently even the traditional playground ball is to be considered dangerous.
- When the rules on a playground sign take an inordinate amount of time to read, the overall message may as well be, "No fun allowed" (Skenazy, 2023).

But what truly constitutes risk? Educator Rusty Keeler implores us to consider the difference between risk and hazard. Risks, he writes, "are situations that a child can perceive and choose whether or not they want to participate. This could be balancing on a log, jumping off a rock, wrestling with a friend, or stepping in mud" (Keeler, 2020, p. 17). These are natural kinds of activities, Keeler says, that belong in children's lives.

A hazard, on the other hand, is something truly unsafe for a child: "situations or objects that the child does not see, cannot make a logical choice about, and that have a definite chance of hurting them" (Keeler, 2020, p. 17). Keeler cites exposed concrete footing on a playground, broken glass, a cliff, dead branches in a climbing tree, cars in the road, and a rock buried in mulch under a piece of climbing equipment as examples of hazards. These, of course, we must protect against.

Associate professor of pediatrics Mariana Brussoni and colleagues (2015) remind us that due to rising concern over child safety and injury prevention, the meaning of the word *risk* has changed over time. Once a neutral term indicating "the probability of a given outcome," it is now associated with negativity and danger. Clearly, this is the case: when I look at the thesaurus for synonyms for *risk*, they include *danger, jeopardy, peril, hazard, menace,* and *threat*.

"Worst-first thinking" is a term Lenore Skenazy, founder of Free-Range Kids, uses often. It describes our tendency to imagine only the worst possible outcome in every situation, and it's a concept that has become ubiquitous in our society. I believe it's incumbent upon us, as early childhood professionals, to counterbalance this kind of thinking.

WHY RISKY PLAY?

There are two childhood memories related to play that remain strong in my mind. The first is mounting the front steps of my house and then climbing to the flat cement ledge above the top step. From there, I jumped to the narrow, concrete, walled-in area below. It was a long and scary jump. It was terrifying, in fact, and if I thought too long about doing it I'd back down. So, I climbed quickly and jumped! This memory reminds me of the kind of kid I was, of the risks I was willing to take, and of the kind of bravery those risks required. Now, when I find myself afraid of taking a risk, or of a new situation, I bring that kid to mind, and realize she's still inside of me.

The second memory is of an older girl in the neighborhood teaching me how to do cartwheels down the middle of the street. They didn't come easily to me, and I practiced repeatedly until I finally got them right. What a sense of accomplishment I had! This memory helps me recall just how persistent I can be—and that persistence pays off. Yes, I could have injured myself doing either of these two activities, but I'm very glad that didn't stop me because bravery and persistence are two traits no one should be without.

Life requires risk. Not every adult will choose to go into outer space, for example, or to participate in bungee jumping. But making a commitment—either to a person or a career—requires taking a risk. Filling out a college application requires risk. Speaking up to right a wrong requires risk. Even walking into a new social situation requires an element of risk. These are just a handful of examples of the kind of chances adults take. However, well before children reach adulthood, risk is an inherent part of their lives. It's risky to approach another child in search of friendship. Raising one's hand in class requires risk. It takes a risk to try something you've never done before, like learning to swim or joining in a new game.

The truth is that children are *meant* to be risk-takers. Nature made them that way, while also providing them with the ability to know just how far to push the boundaries. There are infinite benefits to allowing children to take risks, and there are infinite problems resulting from a lack of opportunity to do so. Children who grow up afraid of and avoiding risk will not become risk-takers later in life. Imagine the risk-aversive adult who must choose whether to leave an unsuitable job and seek a better one, to move to a new location, or even to walk into an unfamiliar social situation. The risk-aversive adult is unlikely to become an investor, an entrepreneur, or a leader. The risk-aversive adult will likely struggle with problem solving, as it involves the possibility of making the wrong choice.

There is also a connection between risk and resilience. The latter involves the ability to anticipate and respond to uncertainty. But those uncomfortable with risk are equally uncomfortable with uncertainty. And if there's one thing we know, it's that life doesn't come with certainty.

Moreover, those who haven't taken risks will not learn how to assess them. Conversely, children who have been trusted to use construction tools or to jump from swings and climb up slides become aware of potential pitfalls. They learn how to judge the width of a mud puddle and determine whether it's possible to leap from one side to the other. They learn which tree branches can support them and which aren't worth the gamble. These are the experiences that keep children safer! As Hanscom (2017) reports, when an elementary school principal in New Zealand eliminated all rules from recess, allowing children to scale fences and climb trees, among other things, there was a *drop* in injuries.

Brussoni and colleagues (2015) cite studies demonstrating that experience with risks in childhood may also assist with risk assessment related to decisions about substance use, relationships, and sexual behavior in adolescence. Following are additional benefits that have been associated with risk-taking in childhood.

- Dodd and Lester (2021) hypothesize that exposure to risk—and in particular what they call adventurous play—can help increase children's ability to cope and decrease their potential for anxiety disorders, half of which they tell us begin before the age of 11.
- Children who learn to take risks discover they can manage and overcome their fear.
- Children who succeed at risk-taking develop self-confidence.
- Because frequently there are decisions to be made during risk-taking ("Are the branches sturdy enough?" "Is the puddle too wide?" "Can I make that jump?"), it helps children develop decision-making skills.
- Bisnath (n.d.) writes that, in risky play, children engage in such prosocial behavior as communicating, negotiating, and cooperating and improve such executive-functioning abilities as goal setting,

increased attention span, planning, judgment, and spatial working memory.

All these traits are essential to a healthy life. And it's important to remember that the ability to take risks, as with most other skills, must begin to develop in early childhood. If we adults prevent children from taking risks—physical or otherwise—they will not suddenly acquire the ability simply because they've physically matured.

PUTTING THEORY INTO PRACTICE

Sandseter (2007) defined six categories of risky play. They are:

1. Play with great heights. Examples include climbing, of course, but also jumping from a high surface, crossing a jungle gym, and hanging and swinging on monkey bars.
2. Play at high speed. Children love speed, whether it involves running, riding, or sledding.
3. Play with harmful tools. These could include such kitchen tools as knives or mallets and such construction tools as hammers, nails, and saws.
4. Play near dangerous elements. Fire, ice, and deep water are examples.
5. Rough-and-tumble play. Wrestling is the most common type of rough-and-tumble play. (We'll cover this in the next chapter.)
6. Play where the children can "disappear" or get lost. When children play hide-and-seek, they often are out of sight of adults and other children and enjoy the "danger" of being hidden and on their own.

Mariana Brussoni (2017) wrote that "it's not up to parents or experts to decide what is risky play for a particular child. Rather, children need to be given the mental and physical space to figure out the appropriate risk levels for themselves: far enough that it feels exhilarating, but not so far that it becomes too scary."

Given this fact, this section will not suggest specific activities. Rather, it will offer suggestions for how we adults can surmount our fear-based thinking and allow children the freedom they need to determine their limits.

Children *love* risky play and naturally want to test their boundaries. It's exciting! So, if we're to put theory into practice, our first objective is to *allow* children to test their boundaries. If you feel a "be careful" bubbling up, hold it back. It may take a while to break the habit, but you will with effort. The phrase may slip out the first few times, after which you'll hear it and wish you could take it back. Soon, however, you'll first hear it in your mind and will be able to refrain from saying it aloud.

We also must keep ourselves from interfering in other ways; for example, by redirecting, joining in, narrating, or even applauding the play (Keeler, 2020). Yes, we can and should observe, but we must do so unobtrusively. If we become concerned about the potential for danger, Dr. Brussoni (2017) recommends waiting 17 seconds before stepping in so children have the chance to work things out on their own.

Research professor Peter Gray (2014) has written extensively about children and play. Where risky play is concerned, he assures us that "children are highly motivated to play in risky ways, but they are also very good at knowing their own capacities and avoiding risks they are not ready to take, either physically or emotionally. Our children know far better than we do what they are ready for." We must learn to trust that.

Additionally, we must not overreact should a child stumble, fall, or get hurt. I once witnessed a mother become hysterical when her young daughter fell off a swing that was fewer than 12 inches off the ground. This woman literally screamed at full volume as she raced toward her child. Twenty years later, the child, now a young woman, became the victim of debilitating panic attacks. Fast-forward another 10 years, and anxiety had so incapacitated her that she ended a promising career as a photographer and now rarely leaves her home. Naturally, it was not the one incident described here that incapacitated her; that was merely representative of the ongoing dynamic between mother and child, which I personally witnessed. This individual's childhood and adolescence were filled with overreactions and overprotectiveness, which eventually rendered her unable to live a normal life. Whether or not children are experiencing overprotectiveness at home, we must do our best not to allow it to become part of their experience with us in early childhood learning environments.

Perhaps the best advice comes from Rusty Keeler (2020):

> . . . change does not have to happen in big ways overnight. Little by little is a-ok. In fact, small steps are the best way to get going . . . so make the first steps easy, small, barely noticeable. You don't need to give kids saws, hammer and nails to get the play going. Try putting out a cardboard box or two and stepping back to see what happens. Let the play go a teeny further than you might have previously. Watch what happens. Make mental notes. (p. 23)

Keeler reassures us that once we cross that line and realize everyone is okay, it will be easier to do it again. He also recommends that we adults practice what I'm going to call "benefits-first thinking." In other words, as the children are engaging in adventurous play, instead of envisioning the potential danger, we think about all the rewards the children are reaping.

RECOMMENDED RESOURCES

- *The Coddling of the American Mind: How Good Intentions and Bad Ideas Are Setting Up a Generation for Failure* by Greg Lukianoff and Jonathan Haidt. These authors provide considerable evidence that overprotection does more harm than good.
- Lenore Skenazy's *Free-Range Kids: How Parents and Teachers Can Let Go and Let Grow*, as well as the Free-Range Kids website, https://www.freerangekids.com, can help parents and teachers relax.
- You can listen to a short podcast interview with Rusty Keeler on BRN. "Risky Child's Play: The Good, the Bad, and the Mostly Good" can be found here: https://www.bamradionetwork.com/track/risky-child-play-the-good-the-bad-and-the-ugly.
- *The Atlantic* article "The Overprotected Kid" (https://www.theatlantic.com/magazine/archive/2014/04/hey-parents-leave-those-kids-alone/358631/) claims a "preoccupation with safety has stripped childhood of independence, risk-taking, and discovery—without making it safer" and shares examples of what can happen when children have access to an adventure playground.
- "Risky Play, Managed Well!" (https://www.bamradionetwork.com/risky-play-managed-well/) is a blog post written by early childhood educator Gail Multop. It offers advice on teaching risk management in an ECE setting.
- AnjiPlay is a philosophy of early education developed in China. Risk is one of its five interconnected principles (the others being love, joy, engagement, and reflection). In their online Parent and Advocates Guide (https://www.anjiplay.com/guide), you'll find answers to the question, "Is risky play dangerous?" You can also see photographs of children engaging in activities that many would consider risky.

PARTNERING WITH PARENTS

Not surprisingly, when it comes to risky play, the most important thing we can do is to help manage parents' fears. It's easier said than done, but the following resources can help.

- "How to Talk to Parents About 'Risky Play'" (https://www.childinthecity.org/2017/09/08/how-to-talk-to-parents-about-risky-play) offers some wonderful information you can share with parents.
- The author of the "How to Talk to Parents About 'Risky Play,'" Dr. Mariana Brussoni, has also created an online tool to help

parents manage their fears and develop a plan for change so their children can have more opportunities for risky play. You can direct parents here: https://www.outsideplay.org.

You may also want to share the risk assessment information with parents. It's important for them to understand that by taking risks children best learn how to assess them. As their children become adolescents and teens, this will help them stand up to peer pressure and make good decisions about such things as substance use or sexual relationships.

Additionally, parents should be aware that children are more likely to sustain injuries in adult-directed organized sports than in their own free play (Gray, 2014). The Centers for Disease Control has called youth sports injuries an epidemic, citing 3.5 million injuries per year in the United States alone (National Council of Youth Sports, n.d.). To my knowledge, there is no epidemic of injuries resulting from risky play.

They say a picture is worth a thousand words. If you share photos or videos of children engaged in such activities as balancing on fallen logs, swinging high, climbing the slide, and crossing monkey bars, parents will see the joy, excitement, and *satisfaction* on their children's faces. Also, if you have them, share stories with parents about how their child has grown in confidence and determination. This will help substitute fear with pride!

Finally, it might be helpful to refer to risky play as "adventurous" play, as do researchers Dodd and Lester, cited earlier. An adventure still holds the potential for risk but sounds less hazardous.

CHAPTER 7

Rough-and-Tumble Play

Rough-and-tumble is yet another aspect of play that has succumbed to adults' fears. Concern about children getting hurt has likely always accompanied this type of play. However, because children were far less monitored in the past, they managed to find a way to engage in rough-and-tumble play. And they engaged in it because it comes naturally to them.

Anthropologist Carl Groos first named this kind of vigorous play in his 1898 book *Play of Animals* and again discussed it in his 1901 book *Play of Man*. But psychologist Harry Harlow was the first to study the science of it. In the 1950s, he described the play of rhesus monkeys—chasing, grabbing, pushing, and tumbling—as *rough-and-tumble* and noted that although the monkeys' faces appeared overly aggressive, their play was not. Further studies determined that rough-and-tumble play occurs among *multiple* species. Kelley and Kelley (2017) tell us this type of play is universal in all mammals, including humans, and has its own dedicated neural networks in the brain. Even wasps and spiders engage in rough-and-tumble play (Jones, 2023).

Although most of us likely haven't seen the play of wasps and spiders, we have witnessed the rough-and-tumble play of kittens and puppies and, thanks to zoos and online videos, bear cubs, otters, pandas, and other creatures. While adults often look upon the rough-and-tumble play of young animals as humorous or adorable, the same type of play among young humans can elicit negative reactions. Teachers and parents worry the children will hurt themselves or others. There is also concern that rough-and-tumble play, particularly when it comes to war and gun play (see Chapter 9), may lead to aggressive behavior and even violent tendencies in children. But experts tell us more harm may come from *preventing* this kind of play than from allowing it (Jones et al., n.d.). In particular, "preventing boys from playful aggression may actually increase the likelihood that any suppressed aggression will manifest itself in less healthy and beneficial ways" (Nagel, 2019).

Engagement in rough-and-tumble play usually begins at around age 2 and tends to peak at age 7 (Jantz, 2022), and although we tend to think of this kind of play as the domain of boys only, girls also engage in it. According to a study published in the *International Journal of Environmental Research and Public Health* (Storli, 2021), boys tend to play with physical contact and girls more often without. Additionally, while the play of boys can be aggressive—and this is considered fun among them—aggression in girls is typically destructive to friendships and, thus, more rarely seen among them (Nagel, 2019). It's important to note, though, that there will always be exceptions. Huber (2017) reports that it's often girls who ask him to bring out the mats for roughhousing, and that both boys and girls are in the mix when the children pile on one another.

Huber (2017) writes that *rough-and-tumble* is a term that now embraces all play using the full body, "including body contact with another individual; body contact with objects; and striking objects with feet, hands, or an object" (p. 12). His definition also involves such solitary activities as running and climbing and most others falling under the heading of big body play. As he says, many such activities are neither rough nor include tumbling. In this chapter, however, we'll focus on what has traditionally been considered rough-and-tumble play, sometimes known as roughhousing: wrestling, pillow fights, piling on, chasing one another, play fighting, and such.

WHY ROUGH-AND-TUMBLE PLAY?

Many of the same benefits garnered from risky play (see last chapter) are acquired in rough-and-tumble play: Children challenge themselves, test their limits, and gain self-confidence and risk-assessment skills. Rough-and-tumble play, specifically, has a considerable impact on executive functioning, as children learn impulse control and how to regulate their emotions. They also develop the prosocial skills that come with cooperation and communication. This is especially the case with nonverbal communication, which not only helps individuals "read" the body language of others but also to express thoughts, feelings, and intentions (sometimes more effectively than they would with words).

Rough-and-tumble play allows children to become more fully aware of their bodies and to explore their personal boundaries, as well as those of others. When a touch meant to be playful is instead painful, children learn how to control their strength and how better to interact with one another. Children—especially boys—who lack this type of interaction won't learn how to regulate feelings of aggression, which develop naturally in children. This statement takes on greater significance when we learn that Stuart Brown, founder of the National Institute for Play, discovered in his interviews with 26 prison inmates that none of the murderers had engaged in rough-and-tumble play as children. Brown states that "rough-and-tumble play and the ability to deal with hostility and still get along with your friends is a fundamental part of both animal and human experience" (Jones, 2023).

Although we may not often consider the role of touch in child development, Frances Carlson contends physical contact can be more important in sustaining life than food and water! In a BRN interview (Carlson, n.d.), she cited research indicating that when children are denied touch, they fail to grow physically and to develop the emotional and social skills they need to succeed in early childhood and in life. In that same interview, Lisa Fiore, director of Early Childhood Education at Lesley University, pointed out that our society offers fewer and fewer opportunities for physical contact. And it's true; children are spending more time in front of screens, being pushed in strollers even as preschoolers, and are discouraged—even prevented—from roughhousing. Without the latter, boys in particular don't have their needs for touch met. Rough-and-tumble play is one of the only socially acceptable ways for boys to experience touch.

Of course, the vigorous nature of rough-and-tumble play also means this type of play contributes to physical development and physical fitness. All the health-related factors of physical fitness—cardiovascular endurance, muscular strength, muscular endurance, flexibility, and body composition—are addressed as children wrestle with or chase each other.

Adults may feel uncomfortable with many of the activities that fall under the heading of *rough-and-tumble play*, but there's no doubt that the skills acquired from it will serve children for a lifetime.

PUTTING THEORY INTO PRACTICE

It's not unusual to be uncomfortable with something if we've had no personal experience with it and, traditionally, girls have had less personal experience with rough-and-tumble play involving physical contact. Early childhood education is a female-dominated profession, which may help explain why this type of play tends to be discouraged—or, at least, not actively encouraged. A study conducted by Storli and Sandseter (2015) determined that "play-fighting and chase games" are the play types most restricted by preschool teachers. Acceptance and support, then, are necessary to put theory into practice. We must accept that the need for roughhousing and superhero play is inherent in children and support their experiences with it because the benefits far outweigh the risks.

Naturally, the risk is what most worries adults. However, having predetermined rules can help alleviate both the worry and the risk. The one guideline Huber (2017) establishes is that the children will take care of each other. You may choose to be more specific, with such rules as

- We will not bite.
- We will not grab above the shoulders.
- We will not hit others with objects.

- We will stop play as soon as someone isn't having fun. (When one player calls "Stop!", everyone stops.)

Limit the rules to just a few and discuss them with the children. Do they believe the guidelines are fair? Are there others they feel are important? I have long contended that children are far more likely to abide by rules they've had a role in establishing.

Another way to ensure the risk is lessened is through observation. If the children are smiling or laughing, they're playing. If a child is crying, frowning, or expressing anger or fear, it's not play. That's when you should ask if everyone is still having fun. If not, it's appropriate to intervene, which can involve anything from reminding the children to be gentle to stopping the play altogether. But that should be a last resort. Children need to learn to play fairly and to resolve their own conflicts, but they won't learn these lessons if their play is overly monitored. Your observation, then, should be as unobtrusive as possible. And as is the case with risky play, you'll want to refrain from saying, "Be careful." The ability to hold back such warnings is a muscle that needs to be exercised; the more you practice it, the stronger it will become.

As with other types of risky play, you'll want to refrain from overreacting if something goes wrong. Even with rules in place, children can get hurt, and your first inclination will be to rush to offer comfort and assistance. But bumps and bruises come with the territory. If the injury isn't serious (and it isn't likely to be), it's a good idea to allow the children involved to offer comfort and assistance to one another. Boys in particular don't get many opportunities to show concern and offer care, but they will if given the chance.

Because rough-and-tumble play is vigorous in nature, it's best to limit it to those times when it's acceptable for the children to be energetic. If this kind of play precedes nap or rest time, for example, the children will struggle with winding down, and there's no need to put anyone through that experience.

How can you encourage rough-and-tumble play? Below are some ideas.

- Bringing out mats signals that all systems are go for wrestling and piling on. You won't need to issue invitations; those who are eager for this kind of play will be there in a heartbeat. Huber (2017) recommends that children roughhouse on their knees unless there is quite a lot of space for it. Also, the area around the mat should be clear of hard objects.
- Make multiple pillows available for pillow fights.
- Make such soft objects as pool noodles and Nerf balls available for roughhousing that involves striking one another.
- If you live in an area where the trees shed their leaves in the fall, invite the children to gather the leaves into piles and then to jump in.

- Male teachers are more likely to engage in play involving body contact. If you're female, support it! And, if full-body contact is not something you're comfortable with, tickling games are a great substitute.

Chasing that falls under the heading of *rough-and-tumble play* typically involves one child spontaneously pursuing others. However, you can also arrange tag games that help fulfill the desire for children to pursue each other and experience physical contact. Blob Tag is described in Chapter 3 and Shadow Tag Chapter 4. Below are other possibilities for rough-and-tumble play.

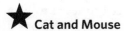
Cat and Mouse

This simple game of tag involves plenty of action, constant participation from everyone involved, and a lot of fun. One child is designated as the cat, while the rest of the children act as mice. The object of the game is for the cat to catch a mouse. The mouse who is tagged becomes the cat, and the original cat becomes a mouse. The new cat can tag anyone except the child who was most recently the cat, which allows all children to be more involved in the game.

Turtle Tag

This game is played like the traditional game of Tag, with two exceptions: First, if a child is being chased, she can be "safe" by lying on her back like an upside-down turtle, and, second, the game is timed. If the child who is "It" hasn't tagged someone in a certain amount of time (for example, a minute and a half), at the sound of your signal, the person who is "It" should get into the "turtle position." You then choose another child to be It.

Elbow Tag

The players are paired off, with all but two of the children linking arms. Of the two without arms linked, one is "It" and the other is the person "It" is going to chase. At your signal, everyone starts to run. The child whom "It" is chasing tries to hook onto one of the linked pairs. If he manages to link his elbow with someone else's, he and the child he's linked with becomes a new pair, and the child on the opposite side of them is set free to become the child being chased. If "It" tags the child being chased before she can link with someone, she and "It" reverse roles. But, because they're in such close proximity at this point, an immediate tag-back wouldn't be fair. So, the game should pause temporarily, allowing "It" and the "chasee" to separate. You then give the signal for everyone to start running again.

 **Reverse Tag**

Everyone but "It" counts to five, during which time "It" runs as far away from the group as possible. Then, all the other children chase the person who is "It." The child who manages to tag "It" then becomes "It" and must run away from everyone else.

RECOMMENDED RESOURCES

- Rough-and-tumble play is the subject of two podcasts on BRN: "Why Rough and Tumble Play Is Really Good" (https://www.bamradionetwork.com/track/why-rough-and-tumble-play-is-really-good/) and "Pillow Fights, Wrestling, and Piling on: Good for Kids?" (https://www.bamradionetwork.com/track/pillow-fights-wrestling-and-piling-on-good-for-kids/).
- To see Mike Huber and children in action, you can watch a short video here: https://www.youtube.com/watch?app=desktop&v=jQqoGZu_DFU.
- To understand the benefits of touch in children's lives, I recommend Frances Carlson's *Essential Touch: Meeting the Needs of Young Children* (NAEYC, 2006).

PARTNERING WITH PARENTS

As with any type of "risky" play, rough-and-tumble is a tough sell with parents. This kind of play may be especially worrisome because it *appears* to have greater potential for harm. So, just as I recommended for risky play (Chapter 6), your priority will be to allay parents' fears and help them understand the many benefits of this type of play. You can also help them understand that some aggression is *natural* in children, and rough-and-tumble play—particularly war, gun, and superhero play—will not lead to more aggression. Rather, the opposite is a possibility; if children—especially boys—have no outlet for their natural aggression, they may seek it later in less positive ways. Additionally, you can offer reassurance by explaining the precautions you have put in place.

If possible, invite parents to visit when children will be engaged in rough-and-tumble play. Alternatively, as I recommended with risky play, you can let photos and/or videos tell the tale. Huber (2017) shares the story about a game involving two children at a time tumbling, tickling, rolling, and pushing each other on a mat. The remaining children cheered, "Let's go wild!" (the name of the game), while they waited their turn. The directors of the childcare center where this game was played sent a video of it to the parents, who could see for themselves there was nothing to worry about. Moreover, they were moved by the children's joy and excitement.

Nagel (2019) encourages fathers, who typically play more vigorously with their children, to engage in rough-and-tumble play with their children in order to help regulate their behavior and emotions. Following are his suggestions for parents.

1. Do allow for playful aggression but don't intervene; instead monitor the behavior to ensure all participants are enjoying themselves.
2. Do teach [children] how to take turns when needed but don't then make decisions for them . . . autonomy helps to build social skills.
3. Do watch for those [children] who may not wish to engage in playful aggression but don't stop others from doing so; instead find alternatives for those who would rather do something else.
4. Do engage in playful aggression but don't dictate how everything is done; let the child makes some choices and change the rules when appropriate . . . this helps to teach responsibility and further develop social skills.
5. Do learn to relax when you see playful aggression and don't overestimate any perceived dangers . . . [children] will let you know when they are safe and happy or not in their play.

CHAPTER 8

Cooperative Play

Emphasizing cooperation over competition can be a tough sell, more so in some areas of the world than in others. It's certainly true in the United States. During live presentations, I occasionally prefaced my negative comments about competition in early childhood with a request that the audience not throw tomatoes at me. I was joking, but I might not have been if there were actual tomatoes available.

I realize that to a certain extent, competition has always had a place in both education and parenting. Students have long competed for good grades, and parents have long compared their child's growth, intelligence, talents, and grades with those of the neighbors' children, even if simply in their own minds. Being competitive is seen as the way to succeed in a "dog-eat-dog" world, and it seems belief in such a world is stronger than ever these days. The extent to which competition has become entrenched in education and parenting is unprecedented. A physical education teacher once told me he had eliminated most competition from his elementary PE program but not all of it. His reason, as he stated it, was: "These kids are going to have to compete every day for the rest of their lives."

But is that true? This one comment perfectly illustrates adults' conviction that competition is pervasive in life, even in childhood.

I don't know the origins of this kind of thinking, but much of the competitive attitude in education can be traced first to 1957, when the Soviet Union won the space race with the launch of *Sputnik 1* and policymakers decided education reforms were needed to make the United States more globally competitive (Lyons, 2022, p. 18).

Then came the 1983 publication of "A Nation at Risk: The Imperative for Educational Reform." This document sounded an alarm about supposed declining educational standards. The perception that U.S. students were falling behind those in other countries was the impetus for an education system centered on standards, testing, and accountability. Even though much of the report later was proven to be misleading and misguided (Kamenetz, 2018)— and its resulting policies have failed to improve learning outcomes (Sahlberg & Doyle, 2019)—competition and accountability prevail. No Child Left Behind and Race to the Top, along with current education policies, pit students, teachers, and administrators against one another and have given rise to the widespread myth that "earlier is better."

This myth has become deeply embedded in our society and is largely responsible for parents' fervent insistence that their children be involved in academics, athletics, and other extracurricular activities at the earliest possible age. They see this as the path to their children's future success. This myth is also responsible for pushed-down curriculum. According to researchers from the University of Virginia, kindergarten has become the new 1st grade (Bassok et al., 2016), meaning that today's kindergarten children are expected to meet standards previously set for 1st-graders. But much of what I hear indicates it's even worse than that: Preschool children are currently asked to meet what were previously kindergarten standards.

Today's children are under tremendous pressure to meet unrealistic expectations, expectations for which they are not yet developmentally equipped. Child development, it seems, is not taken into consideration. Despite the facts that child development cannot be accelerated; young children are not cognitively, socially, emotionally, or physically ready for competition; and education reform has failed, competition still prevails.

IS IT REALLY A DOG-EAT-DOG WORLD?

Will children really have to compete *every day of their lives*? Is that even possible? Is it truly so combative out there? Is the world primarily "every man for himself?" Is it a place that requires us to prepare our children to battle, rather than belong? To clash, rather than collaborate? To see everyone else as foe, rather than friend?

I simply don't see the world in that way. After all, there aren't, for example, only six As allotted per classroom, requiring the children to engage in a battle to attain one. If kids want good grades, they must work for them—not in a way that causes someone else to fail, but by doing their own personal best. If they want to get into a good college, the same principle applies. Yes, there are only so many placements at each university, but if kids have put forth the appropriate effort, learned a good work ethic, and are people with character, regardless of whether they get into their first or fourth choice of schools, they're going to be just fine. More than fine!

The same pertains when individuals apply for the job of their dreams. Yes, they're competing against other applicants, but it's unlikely they even know who those other applicants are and what they bring to the table. Nor can they be aware of every factor involved in the selection process. All they can do in that situation is to, once again, be their own personal best. As former physical education professor Bob Hautala once said to me, "On an individual basis, head-to-head competition is rarely encountered in the real world."

If we stop to think about it, we realize he's right. There are far more opportunities over the course of a lifespan to cooperate and collaborate than there are to compete. After all, we need to learn to get along and function with family members, spouses, colleagues, neighbors, and other members of the local and global community. All of that requires cooperation!

Moreover, today's employers are looking for people who are adept at working well with others. According to Indeed.com (Herrity, 2023), this is one of the top qualities that employers are seeking. They write: "Though not every job requires collaboration, the ability to work effectively and harmoniously in a group is a strength that employers want their employees to have. In fact, they will likely ask you how you function in a team during the interview process, so come prepared with an anecdote that highlights your ability to compromise and collaborate."

Obviously, this is contrary to the assumption that pitting children against one another is necessary preparation for surviving in the world of college and beyond. Children who come to see every other child as direct competition will not be prepared for a future in which they'll have to negotiate, cooperate, and collaborate.

Many argue that competition is "human nature," but there's much debate as to whether this is true. While Freud alleged competition is innate, anthropologist Margaret Mead argued that a competitive drive is learned (Sklyar, 2017). Then there are those who contend it's a combination of nature and nurture.

Like Margaret Mead, I tend to believe we *teach* children to be competitive—with games in which one player prevails and everyone else "loses," and by asking children, "Who won?" instead of, "Did you have fun?" My belief is strengthened by the fact that in some cultures, this is not the case. I'll never forget the essay in which Nicholas Kristof (1998) described his experience of trying to teach Musical Chairs to 5-year-old Japanese children. One girl, who had politely stepped out of the way to allow another child to have a seat, expressed her disbelief that good manners were to be punished—that being rude was the point of the game.

WHY COOPERATIVE PLAY?

When children see that competition is what adults value, that is what they come to value as well. However, given a choice, most young children prefer cooperative activities to competitive ones (Gray, 2022). That alone should be reason enough to support cooperative play. But there are other reasons as well.

Alfie Kohn (1992), in what is undoubtedly the definitive book on competition versus cooperation, tells us that the latter:

- Is more conducive to psychological health
- Leads to friendlier feelings among participants
- Promotes a feeling of being in control of one's life
- Increases self-esteem
- Results in greater sensitivity and trust toward others
- Enhances feelings of belonging
- Increases motivation

Lyons (2022) tells us simply that cooperation makes work easier and creates social bonds. She writes, "Stop for a moment to appreciate how integral these effects of cooperation are to peace, happiness, and prosperity" (p. 25).

When children cooperate rather than compete, good things happen. If given a chance to work together toward a solution or common goal—whether creating a game, collaborating on a jigsaw puzzle, or bouncing cotton balls on a parachute to create a "snowstorm"—they know they each contribute to the success of the venture. Each child realizes they play a vital role in the outcome, and each accepts the responsibility of fulfilling that role. They also learn to become tolerant of others' ideas and to accept the similarities and differences of other children.

Furthermore, cooperative activities seldom cause the feelings of inferiority that can result from the comparisons made during competition. On the contrary, because cooperative and noncompetitive activities lead to a great chance for success, they generate greater confidence in children.

Many years ago, I was asked to consult for *Sesame Street*. Their upcoming season was to be based on games, so I prepared a presentation on cooperation versus competition. When I finished, the former head writer raised his hand and asked, "If children never lose, how will they learn to lose?" While learning to lose, or fail, offers important life lessons about persistence and resilience, these lessons are not the specific object of cooperative play (although they can result from cooperative play). In life, there will be multiple opportunities for children to learn about losing. But a *lot* of losing in childhood can result in feelings that last a lifetime. It certainly can lead to learned helplessness, the belief that one is powerless. None of us want children to grow up with that belief.

Nor do we want children to become overly accustomed to winning or to being told repeatedly that they're a winner. I saw this manifest itself in a teenager who participated in a dance competition. She placed second, and I watched in shock as she threw the second-place trophy at the judge. Nothing but first place was good enough for her.

Between these two extremes is the child who has experienced enough success—and possesses enough confidence and self-esteem—to understand that sometimes you win and sometimes you don't. When we give children unconditional acceptance and an early sense of security, they are better prepared to deal with rejection and to face problems and disappointments head-on. This is what occurs with cooperative play. And this is what helps children learn to lose gracefully when the occasion arises.

If cooperation plays a larger role in life than does competition, shouldn't we focus on the former in our work with young children? Or perhaps a better question is: Don't we want to strive for a world in which cooperation plays a larger role than competition? If the answer to that question is *yes*, then we must ensure that children grow up well versed in cooperation. Early childhood is the time when habits are formed. This is true whether we're talking about good eating habits, physical activity habits, or habits related to social and emotional issues. The ability to cooperate doesn't just appear. It must be fostered from an early age.

If we value community in our learning environments and would like to see a world in which people peacefully and productively coexist, cooperative activities experienced in the early years are the starting point.

PUTTING THEORY INTO PRACTICE

There are so many possibilities when it comes to cooperative play. For instance, when children are given the opportunity to build together, to make up their own games, or to create scenarios in a housekeeping or dramatic-play center, cooperation is involved—"You be the doctor, and I'll be the nurse." But there is also no shortage of cooperative games you can play with the children. Those I've shared below are intentionally cooperative. However, you can also modify some traditionally competitive games so they become cooperative games.

Musical Chairs, for instance, can easily be adapted so it is no longer a zero-sum game in which one child wins and everyone else loses (and most of the children end up standing around). With Cooperative Musical Chairs, some of the rules remain the same: The children circle the chairs while music plays, and one chair is removed with every round. Children, however, are not removed. Instead, they must find a way to *share* the remaining chairs, even when there's only one left.

If you've ever played the traditional version, you know that children are desperate not to be eliminated. Sitting against the wall and watching everyone else continue to have fun is a miserable experience. To avoid that, children will often push others out of the way to get to a seat. (I've also witnessed worse.) With Cooperative Musical Chairs, however, the atmosphere is very different. The children are laughing and giggling as they collaborate to solve the problem of the decreasing number of chairs. You can practically see their brains at work! All of that provides reason enough to modify the traditional version.

Of course, with any kind of problem solving, the first solution is usually the most common one. In this case, that means one child may sit, while the others try to climb aboard that child's lap. If you witness such a scenario, acknowledge that it is indeed one possible solution. Then invite the children to find another way and start again. Each time you issue such an invitation, the children will become more creative with their responses and more confident in their creativity and problem solving.

In my work with the little ones, I witnessed two solutions to sharing a single chair that stand out in my mind. The first was when every child placed "one big toe" on the last chair, thus successfully completing the challenge. But my favorite solution was when one child sat on the last chair and the remaining children formed a human chain by holding hands and linking to the seated child. *That*, to me, is the way the world should work.

Heads-up: If the children are accustomed to playing the traditional version, you will at first have to convince them the new version isn't going to leave anybody out!

The following are some group cooperative games. You'll note that all are circle games. In early childhood settings, circle times bring about a sense of community—of belonging—that no other group formation offers. Each individual in a circle is significant. Among the social skills fostered "in the round" are recognition of others and both verbal and nonverbal communication. Whether the children are holding hands or simply sitting or standing side by side, the circle is a symbol of their togetherness. It allows participants to see and hear everyone else. When everyone in the circle moves or sings in synchronization, this enhances the feeling of belonging, even for the child who may be shy or uncomfortable in other group activities.

Because building community is an objective of these games, in addition to the acquisition of cooperative skills, all the games fall under the content area of social studies. If there are also concepts belonging to other content areas, I've cited those as well.

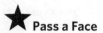

Pass a Face

The children sit or stand in a circle, and one child begins by making a face that is "passed" to the child to the right or left. That child makes the same face and passes it along in the same direction. When the face has been passed all around the circle, the process is repeated, with a different child beginning and a different face made. Moving sequentially around a circle contributes to mathematical knowledge. Being able to physically replicate what the eyes see contributes to the ability to write, part of emergent literacy.

 **Pass a Movement**

This is similar to the preceding game, but the children form a standing circle and pass an action. The first child might, for instance, bend at the waist and straighten. Each child in succession must then do the same.

 **This Is My Friend**

In this game, adapted from Orlick (2006), the children stand in a circle holding hands, and one child raises the arm of the child to the right or left, saying, "This is my friend." The child whose arm has been raised announces her name and then raises the arm of the next child in the circle, saying, "This is my friend." The process continues all the way around the circle, with arms remaining raised, until the last child has had a chance to say his name. When that happens, the children take a deep bow for a job well done.

A variation of this game is for the children to introduce each other. For instance, a child raises the arm of the child to her right or left and says, "This is my friend [Michael]." The original version is a wonderful activity at the start of the year, when the children are becoming familiar with each other. You can introduce the variation once all the children know one another.

 **Group Balance**

The children form a standing circle and place their hands on the shoulders of the children on each side of them. They must then maintain a steady balance through the teacher's invitations to lean forward, backward, left, and right; rise onto tiptoes; stand on one foot; and so on. Balance, of course, falls under the content area of science.

The following games are cooperative partner activities.

 **Mirror Game**

Partners stand facing each other. One partner performs a series of single movements in slow motion (standing in place), which the second partner mirrors. After a while, partners reverse roles. The object is not to try to trick each other but to resemble a mirror reflection as closely as possible. This game falls under the content area of art because it requires children to physically replicate what their eyes are seeing, and that's what artists often do. It similarly addresses emergent literacy because when learning to write, children again must physically replicate what their eyes see.

 Shadow Game

This is similar to the Mirror Game, but it involves one partner standing with their back to the second partner. The child in front performs various *traveling* movements that the partner behind must shadow. Again, partners eventually reverse roles, so both have a chance to lead and follow. In addition to requiring physical replication of what the eyes are seeing (art and emergent literacy), *in front of* and *behind* are mathematical concepts, and shadows are a science concept.

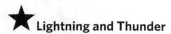 Lightning and Thunder

Partners decide who is first going to be lightning and who is first going to be thunder. (If the children are not yet developmentally ready for this, you can assign each. For example, you might assign the shorter of the two to begin as lightning.) On your signal, the partners separate and begin moving around the room or outside area, keeping their eyes on one another. The partner acting as lightning will periodically "strike" (move like lightning). And because thunder is the sound that follows lightning, the partner acting as thunder will respond by moving in a way they feel depicts thunder. After a while, partners reverse roles. Because this game addresses elements of nature, it falls under the content area of science.

 Switcheroo

Partners stand back-to-back. You then call out the name of a body part or parts (for example, "hands" or "knees"). The children then turn to face each other, briefly bring together those body parts, and then immediately get back-to-back again. When you call out "switcheroo," the children find new partners, and the process starts again, with you calling out different body parts. When the children are more experienced, to add an additional challenge to the activity, call out nonmatching parts too (for example, "hand to knee"). To make the process of finding a new partner less stressful, assign an area—typically the center—as "lost and found." Tell the children that if they can't find a new partner they should head to lost and found. The body-part identification involved here falls under the content area of science.

RECOMMENDED RESOURCES

The cooperative-games movement had its heyday in the 1970s and 1980s. Unfortunately, that means many of the resources I called upon earlier in my career are now out of print. Terry Orlick's (2006) book, however, is still available, as is Suzanne Lyons's (2022) book, which has a section on games for early childhood.

Two other possible activity resources include my *Great Games for Young Children*, which includes sections on both circle and cooperative games, and *Everyone Wins*, Third Edition: *Cooperative Games and Activities for All Ages* by Ba Luvmour and Josette Luvmour.

I also highly recommend Alfie Kohn's *No Contest: The Case Against Competition*.

PARTNERING WITH PARENTS

- Parents want their children to succeed. Although that will have different meanings for different families, success often translates to financial well-being. For that reason, it's important that parents know the ability to work well with others is a *top priority* for employers.
- Share the following short, bullet-pointed list citing the positive benefits of those with cooperative skills, versus the negative characteristics created by competition.
  » Increased self-esteem
  » Enhanced pro-social skills
  » More sensitivity and trust toward others
  » Heightened motivation
  » Greater appeal to potential employers
- Choose some of the cooperative activities cited in this chapter to share with families. A parent and child, a pair of siblings, or a child and playdate can enjoy the partner activities, while whole families or groups of friends can participate in the group games.

CHAPTER 9

Dramatic Play

Dramatic play goes by many names: sociodramatic play, pretend play, fantasy play, and make-believe play. But whatever title we give it, this type of play involves children as "actors" taking on roles and acting them out. Young children are naturals at dramatic play. Not only do they lack the self-consciousness many adults feel, but, also, because schooling has yet to encourage conformity, their creativity is at a peak stage (Anthony, n.d.). Their imagination is free to run wild, and it does!

In dramatic play, we often witness children portraying "scenarios and roles that reflect the social world in which they live" (Kemple, 2017). This essentially allows them to rehearse for adulthood. We see them portraying domestic scenes, playing "doctor" (particularly if they've just had experience with one), or taking on the roles of such heroes as police officers and firefighters. Frequently, these scenarios are a way for children to cope with emotional situations. During the pandemic, parents and educators observed many children acting as doctors, nurses, and patients. If a child has had an unhappy outcome related to a personal situation, they will often change that outcome in their play. This offers a sense of control where none previously existed.

But as we know, children are also adept at transforming themselves into nonhuman entities. Pretending to be an animal is a particular favorite in dramatic play. Perhaps because they're both similar to and different from humans, to children, animals are endlessly fascinating and, thus, worthy of imitation. The ability to take on the characteristics of animals makes it clear that children don't necessarily need personal experience with something to portray it. They take their ability to imagine one step further when they "become" such otherworldly creatures as a superhero, a dinosaur, or a monster.

It is beyond sad—and not at all acceptable—that many early educators have been directed or have chosen to rid their classrooms of housekeeping and other dramatic play centers due to the mistaken notion that academic instruction is more important than play. Fortunately, play advocates are working hard to reverse this trend.

WHY DRAMATIC PLAY?

Adults find it adorable when a little one playing restaurant asks for their order, or when another imagines himself as a horse. And it is adorable. But role-playing goes far beyond cuteness. Play of this kind offers young children innumerable benefits. Among them is the opportunity to stretch the imagination, to find new ways to be and think.

Creativity, I've long felt, receives a great deal of lip service but not nearly enough respect. Perhaps it's because creativity is often associated with the arts only. While most adults are happy to take advantage of the arts—attending movies and concerts, reading novels, or visiting museums—it seems too few parents want their children to become artists, concerned that the financial reward will not be great enough. The world would be lost without its artists, but as I often point out, creativity is not the domain of artists alone.

Franken (2006) defines creativity as "the tendency to generate or recognize ideas, alternatives, or possibilities that may be useful in solving problems, communicating with others, and entertaining ourselves and others." Without creativity in medicine, for example, there would be no cures for illnesses. Without creativity in technology, there would be no innovations that make our lives easier. (When I first began writing, it was on a typewriter, so I'm exceedingly grateful the computer was invented!) Without creativity in business and industry, there would be no new products and services. Without creativity in the classroom, children would not learn problem solving and critical thinking. And without creativity in everyday life, adults would be unable to find a new way to stretch a budget, make a meal from leftovers, or resolve a conflict.

However, there is another vital reason children should develop their creativity. When children can imagine what it's like to be someone or something else, they are experiencing empathy, and empathy is one of the most vital social skills an individual can possess. Empathy allows us to step into others' shoes and connect with them on a deeper level. Aguilar (2018) tells us that empathy "is a precursor to compassion, which is empathy in action—a commitment to doing something that relieves someone else's suffering." Empathy can be extended beyond humans as well. For example, empathy is required if children are to grow up with a healthy respect and concern for all the earth's creatures.

Through dramatic play, young children also experience language development, particularly as it relates to expressive and receptive language. As they create scenes together, children must find ways to express their thoughts and desires, for example, "It's time to open the restaurant. You open the door, and I'll start cooking the pasta." With your assistance, children expand their vocabulary. Salinas-Gonzalez and colleagues (2018) recommend the use of verbal mapping—describing what the children are doing—to introduce new words. This can be especially helpful to dual-language learners.

Dramatic play impacts all developmental domains, but perhaps has the greatest effect on social-emotional development. In addition to the growth of empathy, as Kemple (2017) points out, through dramatic play, children can take on societal roles. It allows them to express and work through their feelings, as evidenced by the role-playing that occurred during the pandemic. And it helps develop self-regulation (Khomais et al., 2019), which, in essence, is the ability to control one's emotions and actions. Livshits (2019) tells us pretend play does this by offering children the chance to practice

- taking on an alternative state of mind and experiment with emotions,
- expressing emotions while in character that may contrast with the child's actual feelings,
- "feeling" and, therefore, managing emotions,
- acting out highly arousing emotional events, and
- negotiating with peers regarding the development of the play.

Through this negotiation, children also become more adept at conflict resolution, a skill that will be necessary throughout life.

WAR, GUN, AND SUPERHERO PLAY

Because it typically involves chasing and fighting, war, gun, and superhero play could well be considered rough-and-tumble play. But drama is at the heart of this kind of play, so I've included it in this chapter.

In Chapters 6 and 7, we discuss risky and rough-and-tumble play, respectively. Parents—and even some teachers—consider both to be hazardous, which means they're generally discouraged or forbidden outright. But of all types of play, perhaps none is considered as taboo—or prohibited as often—as war, gun, and superhero play. Because it involves the use of pretend guns (or swords, or light sabers, as the case may be) and "vanquishing" others, the fear is that this type of play will develop aggression in children, particularly boys. This fear is especially intense when guns have been in the news, particularly as they relate to school shootings.

The experts, however, say there's no correlation between gun play and adult violence (Sole-Smith, 2020). *The Encyclopedia on Early Childhood Development* defines "play fighting" as "verbally and physically cooperative play behavior involving at least two children, where all participants enjoyably and voluntarily engage in reciprocal role-playing that includes aggressive make-believe themes, actions, and words, yet, lacks intent to harm either emotionally or physically" (Hart & Tannock, 2013). This definition should help to allay adults' concerns.

Dramatic Play

What troubles the experts is a zero-tolerance policy for this kind of play. They cite numerous benefits derived from it, including its ability to help children make sense of their world and distinguish between fantasy and reality. Hart and Tannock (2013) report that prohibiting play fighting is especially detrimental to boys and may promote play deficits that unintentionally leave children unprepared for future experiences. Moreover, war, gun, and superhero play are universal in early childhood. When "guns" and gun play are banned, "children find ways to circumvent the ban—they deny that play is really war play (that is, they learn to lie) or sneak around conducting guerilla wars the teacher does not detect (they learn to deceive)" (Levin, 2003). If children are taking such measures, it would seem to indicate not only a real need for this kind of play but also a natural drive toward it.

As much as we may not like to admit it, children can be very aware of what's going on in the world. They may not understand most of what they're absorbing—from the "background noise" of a TV broadcasting the news, or by overhearing adult conversations—but they innately understand there are "bad people" and "bad things." When they play good guy/bad guy, children can work through their feelings and take some control over them. And that feeling of control—the sense that they're powerful and safe—is a must for them.

PUTTING THEORY INTO PRACTICE

Materials, while not absolutely necessary, contribute greatly to dramatic play. Dolls, pots and pans, stuffed animals, and such clothing items as hats and shirts can inspire domestic play. Adding tables and chairs, along with wooden spoons and bowls, may begin to produce scenarios involving a bakery or restaurant.

As you observe the play, should the number of children in the play area decrease, or the children's enthusiasm begin to wane, that's your cue to change things up. Periodically removing and adding materials lends novelty to the children's play, leading them to practice new skills and further stretch their imaginations. It's also important to observe what the children are showing interest in. If the play has turned to restaurants, you could add menus, notepads, and pencils to the area. If the play has turned to grocery shopping, you might add a cash register to the area and empty food boxes, milk jugs, and other such items to shelves.

Kemple (2017) offers an example of this, telling the story of a teacher who noticed the children had begun to "read" aloud to the stuffed animals and to "write" notes, which they placed in envelopes and delivered to cubbies. The teacher, after removing some items from the play area, added a mailbox, a desk and chair, a small rocking chair, and a variety of writing materials and board books. She introduced the new materials on a Monday, and by Friday the children's play had become much more complex.

One way to promote literacy development through dramatic play is to use guided play experiences based on stories you've read several times to the children. Once the story is familiar to the children, you can invite them to depict different characters, expressing the characters' feelings, or to demonstrate various words that play a prominent role in the story. Inviting them to act out the plot can help children begin to understand the connection between spoken language and reading and writing. Salinas-Gonzales and colleagues, (2018) also suggest you make the play area a print-rich setting, adding such items as functional labels, books, and recipes for familiar foods.

When it comes to fostering creativity, your primary role is to let the children's imagination run free. Many adults unwittingly dampen children's creativity by attempting to inject realism into it. I once passed a father and his young daughter in a school hallway just in time to see the child hand her dad a picture she'd drawn and to hear the dad say, "There's no such thing as a blue horse." My heart hurt for the little girl, whose creativity may well have been permanently dampened that day. During the children's dramatic play, we have to suspend disbelief! Saying "There's no such thing as" limits what is possible to a child. Saying "That's not what pots and pans are for" to the child who turns them into instruments limits the possible uses of materials and makes the child feel new ideas aren't acceptable. "I'll show you how to do it" focuses on the "right" way, discouraging experimentation and making the child feel that only adults are able to get it right.

Finally, where gun, war, and superhero play are concerned, Gerard Jones and colleagues (n.d.) caution us to keep from transferring our adult anxieties onto the children. When children pretend to shoot one another, we may experience negative emotions based on the reality of gun violence. But children know they're pretending, and if we make them believe that what they're playing is threatening, we haven't created a safe space for them and for this kind of play.

RECOMMENDED RESOURCES

- There are three excellent podcast episodes about war and gun play on BRN, all of which address children's need for such play and offer advice for teachers.
    - » "War, Gun, and Super-Hero Play: Good or Bad?": https://www.bamradionetwork.com/track/war-guns-and-super-hero-play-good-or-bad/
    - » "Children Playing with Toy Guns and Imaginary Assault Weapons in School. Problem?": https://www

Dramatic Play

> .bamradionetwork.com/track/children-playing-with-toy-guns-and-imaginary-assault-weapons-in-school-problem/
> » "Bang! Bang! Understanding Boys at Play": https://www.bamradionetwork.com/track/bang-bang-understanding-boys-at-play/

- For a deeper dive into war and superhero play, you might want to read *The War Play Dilemma: What Every Parent and Teacher Needs to Know* by Diane Levin and Nancy Carlsson-Paige; *Killing Monsters: Why Children Need Fantasy, Super Heroes, and Make-Believe Violence* by Gerard Jones; or *Under Deadman's Skin: Discovering the Meaning of Children's Violent Play* by Jane Katch.
- NAEYC offers a number of articles relevant to dramatic play. You'll find them at https://www.naeyc.org/resources/topics/dramatic-play.
- An Edutopia article titled "Encouraging Dramatic Play in the Early Childhood Classroom" (https://www.edutopia.org/article/encouraging-dramatic-play-early-childhood-classroom/) recommends a collection of picture books to "guide dramatic play and foster students' literacy and social and emotional skills."

PARTNERING WITH PARENTS

As is the case with any kind of play, you'll want to help parents understand that dramatic play is not frivolous—rather, it is necessary to children's development. Perhaps the most effective way to frame it is that dramatic play helps children rehearse and prepare for adulthood.

Encourage parents to make suitable materials available to their children at home. These might include used clothing, kitchen equipment, or tools. Large empty boxes and other loose parts also inspire dramatic play. Stress the use of open-ended toys and materials, and explain why they're more valuable than those with a single use.

If you use picture books to inspire dramatic play, you might consider creating a lending library for parents, allowing them to borrow one at a time to read at home. Emphasize that encouraging their child to act out the story not only helps with social-emotional development but also promotes literacy skills. The ability to read and write has become increasingly important to parents.

Your most challenging task will be to alleviate parents' fears about war, gun, and superhero play. Explain that while it's acceptable to prohibit toy guns from the home, the gun play itself is both natural and beneficial. They shouldn't worry when children turn sticks and other items into guns, swords, or light sabers. As you discover more about this kind of play, share what you're learning with your parents.

CHAPTER 10

Fine Motor Play

In a piece in *The Guardian* (Weaver, 2018), surgical professor Roger Kneebone lamented that today's medical students and surgeon trainees have spent so much time online and so little time doing things with their hands—citing such hobbies as cooking, woodworking, playing an instrument, or making models—that they don't have the tactile skills needed for a career in medicine or science. He said, "We are talking about the ability to do things with your hands, with tools, cutting things out and putting things together . . . which is really important in order to do the right thing either with operations, or with experiments."

Indeed, early childhood professionals—particularly kindergarten and 1st-grade teachers—repeatedly tell me today's children are lacking in fine motor skills. They're unable to grip a crayon or paintbrush, to use scissors, or to hold a pencil. Even more worrisome—they don't have the strength to tear a piece of paper! This is shocking but not surprising.

As Dr. Kneebone indicated, among other reasons for this troublesome trend, children today are spending far more time swiping and staring than manipulating objects. The next time you go to any public place where adults and children are gathered and waiting—a restaurant, doctor's office, or the back seat of a car—see for yourself: Are children turning the pages of a book or playing with available toys, or are they looking at a digital device?

Furthermore, in many early learning centers, if such old-fashioned objects as blocks and manipulatives get any attention at all, it's still less attention than is given to academics. That's certainly the case in kindergarten and other early elementary grades, where subjects such as art and physical education are too often given short shrift.

Still, despite the lack of fine motor ability, young children are too often expected to grip a pencil correctly and begin writing well before they're ready. As an example, I received an email from the distraught mother of a 3-year-old boy. Her son's childcare center sent home multiple notes complaining that the little boy couldn't sit still or properly grasp a pencil. The mom wanted to know if a 3-year-old should be able to do those things. The answer—to both—is *no*!

FINE MOTOR DEVELOPMENT

Sadly, that little boy's story isn't the only one I've heard that demonstrates either unfamiliarity with or disregard for child development. Following are three points relevant to child and fine motor development of which adult decisionmakers should be aware.

First, motor development occurs

- from the top of the body (the head) to the feet (the bottom),
- from the inside (the trunk) to the outside (the extremities: arms and legs), and
- from the large muscles (trunk, neck, arms, and legs) to the small muscles (fingers, hands, toes, wrists, and eyes).

That means, in short, that gross motor skills/large muscles must develop *prior to* fine motor skills/small muscles. That's not to say we should ignore fine motor skills until the children have reached a mature level in all gross motor skills. But we can't ignore large motor skills and expect that the small muscles will be just fine. Children need big body play—and a lot of it—if they're going to achieve fine motor dexterity.

Secondly, the hand of a preschooler (or even an elementary-age student) is *not* the same as the hand of an adolescent or adult. The young child's hand is considerably smaller, of course, which is a factor in the manipulation of a tall, skinny implement. However, more significant is that the formation of bones in the wrist doesn't begin until a child is 3 years old. Prior to that, there's only cartilage between each finger bone. Ossification—the replacement of cartilage with bony tissue—typically doesn't occur until age 13. This signifies that young children do not yet have the wrist or hand strength that older children and adults do. So, how can we expect them to grasp a pencil and write as older children and adults do?

Thirdly, nature has put a process in place that involves five stages to the development of a proper pencil grip. Children work through each of the following stages:

1. Fisted grip: The child holds the crayon or pencil with the whole hand, in the way a dagger would be held.
2. Palmer grasp: The writing/drawing implement lies across the palm of the hand, with the elbow held out to the side.
3. Five-finger grip: The implement is held between the thumb and four fingers, in almost an upright position.
4. Static tripod grasp: This is a three-finger grasp, with two fingers gripping the implement and the middle finger tucked to the side of it. The fourth and fifth fingers are typically static and not yet tucked into the palm of the hand.

5. Dynamic tripod grasp: This is the mature grasp closest in similarity to that of an adult's grip. It differs from the static tripod grasp in that the fourth and fifth fingers are tucked into the palm and help to stabilize the hand on the writing surface. This is normally achieved by age 5 or 6 but not necessarily in all children.

This is nature's plan, and it cannot be changed. Moreover, we shouldn't try to change it. Pediatric occupational therapist Christy Isbell (2018) contends that if young children are pushed to write before their hands are physically ready, it may negatively affect their desire to express themselves in writing, and they may develop poor handwriting skills that will continue throughout life.

WHY FINE MOTOR PLAY?

Imagine requiring an intricate, lifesaving operation but knowing the only surgeon available is someone with poor fine motor skills! Obviously, not every child with poor motor skills will grow up to be a surgeon. But they may become chefs, dentists, hairstylists, mechanics, or carpenters, all professionals of whom we would require coordinated movements of the hands and fingers.

Hand strength and eye-hand coordination—also part of fine motor development—likewise are needed for any number of athletic endeavors. Whether playing a sport for love or money, hand dexterity is necessary to grip a tennis racket, baseball bat, or golf club; to play pickle ball; to dribble a basketball; and to lace up ice skates. Tactile skills even come in handy in a card game.

And we can't forget the everyday activities involving fine motor coordination. They include

- tying shoes (even managing Velcro, should shoelaces eventually become obsolete);
- buttoning and unbuttoning, as well as zipping and unzipping, clothing;
- manipulating a knife and fork (especially in a public setting);
- picking up small items;
- grasping tongs, a wooden spoon, or a whisk when cooking;
- operating scissors; and
- signing a form with a pen.

Additionally, as I was writing this chapter, I learned of another area negatively affected by poor fine motor skills. A manufacturer of children's classroom equipment told me that today's teachers are unable to handle such tools as screwdrivers and are, thus, no longer able to put this company's equipment together.

All of these—along with many other life and professional activities—require strong fine motor skills: those involving the fingers, hands, wrists, and eye-hand coordination. Unfortunately, despite their many uses in life, fine motor skills are similar to gross motor skills in that they're not highly valued. Once again, it's a case of the functions of the brain being prized over the functions of the body. But it's easy to imagine how unwieldy life could become—how we might lose our *independence*—without these skills.

PUTTING THEORY INTO PRACTICE

Clearly, worksheets requiring children to practice handwriting—even if it's simply to copy letters—before their hands are *ready* for writing make little sense. That sort of practice is also exceedingly boring and so does little to inspire an interest in writing. Gross and fine motor play, on the other hand, prepare children's hands for handwriting and other fine motor skills in the way they were meant to be prepared and in a way that engages children.

It may seem counterintuitive, but I've heard occupational therapists declare that the best way to help children develop pencil grip and handwriting ability is to let them climb trees and hang from monkey bars. Here are three reasons why:

1. Both activities involve the large muscles of the body, which develop prior to the small muscles.
2. Both require a firm grip, thus strengthening the hands and wrists.
3. Both strengthen the shoulders and upper body.

Although we tend to consider only the hands when it comes to writing, shoulder and upper-body strength are also needed so the child has a "stable base of support for . . . hand function" (Isbell, 2018).

Sadly, due to fear of children getting hurt, climbing trees and hanging from monkey bars—once quintessential childhood activities—are now often prohibited. But if you can allow them, I encourage you to do so! If not, be sure the children have plenty of opportunity to push, pull, crawl, and creep, as these skills will also strengthen the shoulders and upper body.

To encourage crawling (using arms and legs to move along the ground on the tummy), which your children may consider "baby stuff," invite them to move as though they're seals, alligators, worms, or snakes. To encourage creeping (moving on hands and knees), invite children to move like such four-legged creatures as kittens, puppies, or turtles. Pretending to be spiders or other insects also serves the purpose.

To promote eye-hand coordination give the children chiffon scarves to toss and catch. Because they float rather than fall, they're wonderful for visual tracking, which is also important to handwriting. The children can start by watching the scarves float to the floor or ground, followed by catching them with their hands. Later, you can invite them to catch the scarves with the back of the hand, a forearm, an elbow, a knee, a foot, or the top of the head.

Obviously, handwriting is not the only fine motor skill we want to hone. We want to foster fine motor development in general. Fingerplays, art activities, dress-up involving buttons and zippers, and cleanup all contribute. And, of course, the materials available in your environment will have a profound effect on fine motor skill development. Isbell (2018) recommends "a wide variety of open-ended materials such as paper, drawing utensils, glue, clay, and small blocks." I would add puzzles, children's scissors and carpentry tools, and such manipulatives as lacing beads, nuts and bolts, and small plastic counters.

The following are more specific activities.

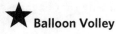

★ Balloon Volley

Like chiffon scarves, balloons are light, move slowly, and are easy to visually track. With this activity, pairs of children volley a balloon back and forth between them. The goal is simply to keep the balloon afloat for as long as they can without either of them touching it twice in a row. To add a math element to the game, ask the children to count each touch.

Once the children are adept at this version, you can challenge them to keep the balloon afloat with any body part *but* their hands.

★ Counting Fingers

Ask the children to each make a fist. Then, as you very slowly count 1-2-3-4-5, the children display their five fingers one at a time. Then reverse, counting backward from five, with the children "closing" one finger at a time. Repeat a few times, gradually increasing the tempo each time. It may be difficult for some children to coordinate, but it's still fun and will come with practice.

★ See My Hands

Invite the children to sit and to move their hands and fingers in the following ways:

Fine Motor Play

- stretching hands and fingers as wide as possible, then bending them into tightly clenched fists
- moving fingers in and out, very fast, then very slowly
- clasping hands together and moving them up and down, in and out, and side to side
- turning hands from front (palms) to back
- making circles with hands without moving the arms

My Hands Can

Invite the children to demonstrate the following, first discussing the meaning of any words that may be unfamiliar to them. How would their hands look if they were:

- mad, scared, happy
- patting an animal
- pushing, pulling
- clapping
- scolding
- fanning
- writing
- painting
- playing guitar, piano
- directing traffic
- waving goodbye

Beanbag Toss

This game promotes both fine motor development and eye-hand coordination. Invite pairs of children to stand about a foot apart and gently toss a beanbag back and forth between them. Explain that, when they're ready (they've gotten very good at tossing and catching from that distance), they can move a little farther apart, and try it.

Rotate It

Parachute play can be excellent for promoting fine motor development. This introductory parachute activity familiarizes children with simply gripping the parachute. The children stand around the parachute and, remaining in place, rotate it by passing it to the right or left. Be sure they rotate it in both directions.

To add another element to the game, you can invite the children to sing the following song to the tune of "Here We Go 'Round the Mulberry Bush":

This is the way we move the chute,
Move the chute, move the chute.
This is the way we move the chute
Here at [name of center or school].

Making Waves

This parachute game gets the arms and shoulders involved, as well as the hands.

Standing around the parachute, the children start by making small up-and-down hand motions that cause little ripples. Gradually, the ripples (hand and arm movements) get larger and larger, until they're gigantic ocean waves.

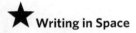
Writing in Space

When the writing is invisible, there's no pressure to get it right. This activity is much more fun than copying letters or words with pencil and paper but still gets children thinking about the straight and curving lines that comprise letters and the way they relate to each other.

Ask the children to imagine the pointer finger on their dominant hand is a piece of chalk, or perhaps covered in paint (in any color they want). They then choose a letter, word, or name they'd like to write and then "write" it—as large as they possibly can—in the air in front of them, using that pointer finger. Repeat several times, gradually decreasing the size of their letter or word.

You can also substitute a brightly colored scarf or short ribbon stick for the finger. This can help children visually track their movements.

RECOMMENDED RESOURCES

- To see X-rays of the hands of a 2-year-old, a 7-year-old, and an adult: https://www.sciencephoto.com/media/302221/view/hand-development-x-ray.
- Christy Isbell's book *Mighty Fine Motor Fun: Fine Motor Activities for Young Children* offers support and tools for teaching fine motor skills.
- Christy is one of three panelists in a 10-minute podcast titled "Fine Motor Skills: What Are They? Why Are They Too Important to

Overlook?" The other two panelists are kindergarten teacher Allison Sampish and early childhood expert Deborah Stewart. You can listen to it here: https://www.bamradionetwork.com/track/fine-motor-skills-what-are-they-why-are-they-too-important-to-overlook/.
- A second relevant podcast is "Introducing Writing Skills to Young Children," with pediatric occupational therapist Angela Hanscom and early childhood expert Amanda Morgan, at https://www.bamradionetwork.com/track/introducing-writing-skills-to-very-young-children/.

Partnering with Parents

- Parents are aware of developmental steps leading to their children walking and talking but not necessarily with the process involved in the development of the hands and fine motor skills. As with gross motor skills, most people, if they even consider it at all, tend to imagine fine motor skills take care of themselves. It's important, therefore, to share information with them. Most essential is that you help parents understand nature has put a process in place that eventually leads to proper pencil grip and handwriting. Parents should also know the process cannot be rushed. Nor should it be unpleasant, as it undoubtedly will be if children are required to learn to write through rote practice and before they're ready.
- Christy Isbell's article, cited in References, would be perfect for including in a cubby, email, or newsletter. You might print X-rays of a child's developing hand, found online, and share that also, along with a brief note indicating what's taking place.
- Recommend that children have access at home to puzzles, child-sized tools, and other materials previously listed. Such art materials as crayons, markers, and paint—to use with hands or brushes—are invaluable.
- Remind parents that there are many everyday tasks the children can do that help promote fine motor development. They include setting the table, pouring milk or cereal, dressing themselves, and picking up toys. Their children can even help with cooking and baking. Using a butter knife to cut cubes of cheese for macaroni and cheese, stirring batter, and mashing potatoes all contribute to the process that leads to an ability to hold a pencil, write, and perform other fine motor skills.

CHAPTER 11

Construction Play

Whether it's building with blocks, Legos, modeling clay, sticks and stones, or sand and water, construction play has long been a staple of childhood. Called *constructive play* by child development expert Jean Piaget and *architecture* by author and educator Ann Gadzikowski (2021), this type of play involves the child's innate desire to create something. Young children everywhere have a natural affinity for building.

Construction play—perhaps especially with blocks—may seem hopelessly old-fashioned to those enamored with the blinking lights, bright colors, and billions of bits of information offered by today's technology. Sadly, many early childhood professionals have chosen or been required to eliminate such "playthings" as blocks from their programs in favor of digital devices and other materials considered more important to academic learning. But how can we disregard the significance of something children are driven to engage in? According to Rubin and colleagues (1983), when given a choice of free play activities, preschoolers choose construction play more than 50% of the time.

Young children are active, experiential learners, and construction play is a hands-on experience that serves as the perfect example of active learning. Creating an onscreen block tower by manipulating a mouse cannot compare to producing one with blocks that can be seen, felt, and even smelled and heard. It's only through these sensory, three-dimensional experiences that children can fully grasp such concepts as shape, size, sorting, spatial relationships, balance, gravity, and others.

WHY CONSTRUCTION PLAY?

The benefits of this type of play, which span all developmental domains, cannot be underestimated. First and foremost, construction play offers children a tangible way to make sense of their world, as they take an idea from something that is abstract to something that is physical and concrete.

The goal of construction play is to make something, but deconstruction serves a purpose as well. Shortly after the twin towers fell in 2001, children were often seen building block towers, only to knock them down. It's how they coped with an event they couldn't understand. Gadzikowski (2021) writes, "There is an undeniable sense of power in destroying something. In the block corner, all children are tiny gods and goddesses. When you can build but also destroy, you have complete autonomy over your own domain" (p. 10). And autonomy is something children seldom have the chance to experience.

Construction play promotes creativity and problem-solving skills, the significance of which are discussed in Chapter 9. Children must first imagine what they want to achieve. That process alone requires problem solving, as the little ones determine which methods and materials will best help them achieve it. But construction includes pitfalls. How can gravity be defied and the materials balanced? What alternatives are there if the materials topple, or if materials don't fit together? Such difficulties require children to employ flexible thinking, which is an essential component in both creativity and problem solving. Children also show incredible perseverance as they work to achieve their desired outcome; this process teaches them an invaluable life lesson about working toward goals.

From an academic perspective, we can see that construction play offers multiple experiences in STEM (science, technology, engineering, and math). Gravity is a science concept, as are balance, stability, cause and effect, and force, all of which must be considered when building. Shape, size, sorting, matching, and spatial relationships fall under the content area of math. When building, children will also count and measure. Together, these concepts and activities comprise an aspect of engineering, which in part involves design and building. And while many assume the "T" in STEM refers to the use of digital devices, that is actually a more modern interpretation of the word. *Technology* is the term used to describe the application of scientific knowledge to solve problems or improve the quality of life. Examples include Stone-age tools, the wheel, buttons and zippers, and automobiles.

As we can see, construction play meets the criteria of STEM. However, it also meets the criteria of STEAM, as the "A" stands for art.

Fine motor development certainly is aided through construction play. As they build, children must grasp and grip materials of different sizes, weights, and textures. They must use both large and small movements of the hands and fingers. As they carefully place, move, and connect materials, eye-hand coordination is promoted. With the exception of art experiences, no other area of play promotes fine motor development as does construction play. (We talk about the importance of fine motor development in Chapter 10.)

Gross motor development and physical fitness are also promoted when construction play involves large objects, as it often does outdoors. As children push, pull, lift—and move over, under, and through—materials, they strengthen their cores and otherwise develop muscular strength and endurance.

Often, children engage in construction play together. When this happens, cooperation (see Chapter 8) is cultivated, as little can be achieved if the children don't work together to reach their goals. Because ideas must be shared and agreed upon, communication skills are also advanced. Additionally, when you scaffold the learning by describing what you're seeing, children acquire new vocabulary. You can further contribute to the children's emergent literacy by adding pencils and notepads to the play area.

Children's construction play benefits you as well. Gadzikowski (2021) writes, "When children build they are making their learning, thinking, and feelings visible in ways that words and conversations can't always communicate. Once we are open to 'reading' a child's structure, we can begin to interpret their play and understand the child more deeply" (p. 118).

Wardle (2000) says that while others may emphasize the social, emotional, physical, and cognitive benefits of construction play, he feels its most significant benefit is that it allows children to be children—to do what children need and want to do.

PUTTING THEORY INTO PRACTICE

Every program should have a block center, whether or not it's required for licensing and accreditation. Sharon MacDonald (2020) writes that she preferred to place her block center in a corner of the room, with a "low-napped rug on the floor to define the space and reduce the noise from falling blocks" (p. 21). She stored the blocks on two open shelves, where the children could easily access them. One shelf was against the wall and the other at the edge of the rug to mark the boundary between the block center and the next center.

You can find advice on the kinds of blocks to buy—and how many—for different age groups in MacDonald's book, *Block Play* (2020). Both she and Ann Gadzikowski (2021) recommend wooden unit blocks as the most versatile.

Other materials that contribute to construction play include these suggestions from Wardle (2000):

- A variety of puzzles
- Mosaic tiles and patterns
- Milk crates, boxes, and other cubes
- Clean pieces of wood of different sizes, shapes, and strengths
- Sticks and stones, leaves, bark, and other natural materials
- Sand and sand toys
- Water and water toys
- Clay, play dough, and other modeling materials
- Wagons and tools to move sand, dirt, and other materials

Just as is recommended with dramatic play, you should refresh construction materials periodically. You don't want to replace too many items at once, or to replace items too frequently, as young children require continuity and repetition. However, removing items that may be getting less use and adding new materials provides the element of novelty the brain seeks. Problem solving, creativity, and learning will all be enhanced by the introduction of new things to work with.

Whatever materials you choose, they should be open-ended, allowing the children's imagination to flourish. Such things as Legos intended to create one item only—for example, a rocket or a race car, as pictured on the box—will stifle the children's creativity and promote the idea that there's only one possible product. As they go through schooling and are faced with rote learning and standardized tests, they'll too often be confronted with the notion of "one right answer." We must do what we can to counterbalance that in early childhood!

Similarly, if we want to foster creativity, problem solving, and perseverance, children need to understand that there are no wrong ways to accomplish tasks. Obviously, if children place blocks in a way that causes them to fall, they have yet to find a "correct" way to balance them. But if you point out that they are doing, or have done, something incorrectly, you'll dampen any enthusiasm they may have had for exploration and discovery. Children may also lose confidence in their ability to find their own answers. It will seem as though only adults have the right ones.

If possible, there should be an area—perhaps a corner of the room or a tabletop—where works in progress can be kept intact. Although the conventional wisdom is that the attention span of young children is short, the little ones can remain interested in a project they enjoy for lengthy periods and should be given the opportunity to extend their play. Just as adults need to feel a sense of accomplishment and completion, so do children.

There is one rule for the construction area that Gadzikowski (2021) insists on, and it's an important one: The person who builds a structure is the only one who can knock it down. It's a rule that won't *always* be obeyed, but if you've discussed it with the children and involved them in the decision-making process, it will be respected more often than not.

RECOMMENDED RESOURCES

- You'll find engineering classroom resources available at https://www.nsf.gov/news/classroom/engineering.jsp.
- *Amag!* (https://a-magazine.org/acerca-de/) is an architecture magazine for children and an Open Educational Resource (OER) for schools.

- Rosanne Hansel has written *Creative Block Play: A Comprehensive Guide to Learning Through Building*. She also wrote "Blocks: Back in the Spotlight Again!" in which she shares research about the ways that playing with blocks increases spatial skills. You can find it here: https://www.communityplaythings.com/resources/articles/blocks-back-in-the-spotlight.
- If you online search "children's books about building," you'll find numerous possibilities. Reading to children about building can enhance their enthusiasm for it, and contribute to their emergent literacy.

PARTNERING WITH PARENTS

Considering all the marketing that toy and technology companies do, claiming their products are educational for children, parents are likelier to be in the market for newer, flashier products than for old-fashioned construction materials. Similarly, parents invested in their children's academic learning may be concerned when their children come home at the end of the day and say they've been playing with blocks. So, it's incumbent upon you to help parents see the value in the "old-fashioned stuff."

It's best if you get out ahead of any potential problem by ensuring parents know and understand your philosophy and why construction play is essential. You can do this with the messaging on your website, or you may choose to communicate in other ways. In her book, MacDonald (2020) offers a sample letter to parents. Along with a brief opening paragraph, the letter includes five bulleted points describing what children learn through block play. The one-page letter concludes with an invitation to parents to see the block center for themselves and, if they want, to build something too.

To reinforce the value of construction play throughout the year, as the children in your program play with blocks and other building materials, take photos and shoot videos! Send them to parents in your emails, newsletters, or whichever app you use to keep in touch with them. Include a few words about what the children are learning and achieving.

If you have enough materials to go around, you might choose to have a lending library, allowing parents to borrow a certain amount for a certain period of time. If you don't have enough for a lending library, encourage parents to have building materials at home. Share your recommendations for materials, along with catalogs or website URLs of companies that you know offer quality products.

You can further involve parents by requesting they donate any recyclable materials to the classroom. Follow up with another invitation for them to come and see how those materials are being used.

CHAPTER 12

Loose Parts Play

Loose parts can be used in construction play. They can be used in dramatic play. They can be employed in both outdoor and indoor play. And they contribute to fine and gross motor development. However, because they have become so popular in early childhood education, loose parts deserve a chapter of their own.

Defined as materials that can be moved, carried, manipulated, and handled in a variety of ways, loose parts can be man-made, natural, purchased, found, or upcycled. Architect Simon Nicholson coined the term *loose parts* to describe "materials with varied properties that can be moved and manipulated in many ways" (Fox & Worth, 2015). He believed that as long as materials could be moved, put together, taken apart, or redesigned, they can be considered loose parts.

Daly and Beloglovsky (2014) offer further criteria for loose parts, writing that, in addition to being mobile, they must be captivating to children and open-ended, providing "multiple rather than single outcomes" (p. 4).

Of course, before Nicholson chose a name for loose parts, children had been using and enjoying them for generations. Materials made of metal, fabric, wood, plastic, glass, ceramics, cardboard, or such natural items as acorns, stones, seeds, and leaves have long been the objects of children's play and inspiration. But only recently have we begun to understand their appeal and value.

WHY LOOSE PARTS PLAY?

In Chapters 9 and 10, I summarize the importance of creativity, and explain the ways in which it's enhanced through dramatic and construction play, respectively. There's no doubt that playing with loose parts—in whatever form it takes—also makes significant contributions to creativity.

Simon Nicholson agreed, citing the vast number of ways it's possible to use and manipulate them. A feather can become a feather *duster*, a bird, or a writing implement (even when a child has never seen a quill pen). Pinecones can become food in dramatic play or pillars in construction play. A piece of blue cloth becomes a baby blanket or a lake. In fact, one day the blue cloth can be the baby blanket and the next the lake! It all depends on the children's imagination. Because there's no right or wrong way to use loose parts (as opposed to many store-bought toys), the imagination is free to soar. That means there are also many chances for problem solving in loose parts play. What will substitute for the branches when they fail to support the roof on the house a child has constructed? What loose part can sufficiently represent a stethoscope in dramatic play about a doctor's office? How many different sounds can be made on that metal pipe? All of this presents multiple opportunities for divergent thinking.

The content areas are amply covered as well. Loose parts found in nature—for example, stones, bark, sand, mud, and branches—contribute to learning in science. And it does so in the way young children learn best, through hands-on experience. As they examine these natural materials, children discover their physical properties. They feel the smooth or sharp edges of a stone and learn about texture (a concept that also falls under the content area of art). They use their senses of sight and touch to discern the differences between sand and dirt. Because their curiosity compels them, they work to discover what lies between the raised layers of bark. They explore and discover the differences between a newly fallen leaf and one that fell earlier and dried. Can one be used in ways the other cannot?

However, learning in the content areas doesn't occur only outdoors. Science discoveries are also made indoors, as when children find that a marble rolls further and in a straighter line than does an empty thread spool, or that a chiffon scarf falls to the ground more slowly than does almost any other loose part. They experience gravity, cause and effect, and momentum when they send various objects through ramps and tunnels they've built with paper towel rolls or PVC pipe. When building those ramps and tunnels, they learn about balance. Why does a magnet adhere to another magnet, a paper clip, or a gear but not to a twig?

There are endless sensory experiences available indoors as well. What do the children hear when they bring a seashell to their ear? Is there a difference between the smell of a dried rose versus that of a dried daisy? What is the difference in texture between a piece of burlap and a scrap of flannel? Why is it louder to strike the table with a PVC pipe than with an empty paper towel roll?

Hirsh-Pasek and Golinkoff (2003) explain that treating objects as though they were something else (known as symbolic thinking) enhances children's language process. For example, vocabulary and communication are expanded when children employ loose parts in their dramatic play and describe what each part represents and how it is to be used. Vocabulary is also expanded when children explore the textures of varying materials and come to fully understand such opposites as *rough* and *smooth* or *hard* and *soft*. They better understand such adverbs as *quickly* and *slowly* when they roll a marble and then a spool. All of this falls under the heading of *emergent literacy*.

Of course, when children work together to create a sculpture, a piece of abstract art, or a soundscape, they collaborate, cooperate, and negotiate. And whether working with others or alone, children acquire such traits as persistence and self-control. All this falls under the content area of social studies.

Math concepts, too, are experienced through loose parts play. Ranheim (2020) tells us, "All the foundational areas of early math can be explored in a playful way using . . . loose parts." Children sort and classify materials. Which are fabric and which are wood? Which are round and which are square? They answer such questions as

- Which is biggest (smallest)?
- Which is lightest (heaviest)?
- How many pieces will they need to use?
- What shape is needed to fit with this other one?
- Is the twig longer or shorter than the branch?
- What is the pattern found in the seashell or piece of bark?

Asking such questions and seeking answers to them is learning born out of curiosity—so much more powerful than the rote learning offered by such things as worksheets and apps. Clearly, loose parts play can help children more fully comprehend concepts and meet standards in every content area. This is active learning at its best.

PUTTING THEORY INTO PRACTICE

The first consideration when offering loose parts is safety. If you're working with children younger than age 4, choking is a possibility when smaller parts are involved. If you're not able to keep a close eye on the children engaging with loose parts, it's best not to provide such small pieces as buttons and beads.

You can begin your loose parts collection by discovering what you already have available. Clearly, you'll find many possibilities outdoors. Are there stones of varying sizes and textures? What have the trees in your outside space dropped to the ground? Have any birds left feathers behind?

If you also take a close look indoors—both at home and at school—you may see items you've never before considered for the children's play experiences. Do you have empty cardboard boxes available? (Young children enjoy these as much as cats do!) Are there scraps of material or skeins of yarn tucked into a closet? Can you find clothespins, empty thread spools, or napkin rings made of wood? For the plastics category, you might look for and gather such items as empty milk jugs, buttons, plastic cups and spoons, and picture frames. Possibilities in the metal category include stainless steel spoons, keys, nuts and bolts, and cookie sheets. Sea glass is a favorite option from the glass category.

Once you've collected what's already available, to find more, you can pop into thrift stores and brake for yard sales. Both are excellent options. Local businesses may also be willing to donate materials you can upcycle.

The secret to inspiring children's creativity and learning is to offer as wide a variety of textures, colors, shapes, and sizes as possible. However, for practical purposes, Haughey (n.d.-b) recommends that you also consider the materials' durability and the storage space you have available. Additionally, she offers the following two suggestions for getting started.

- Start small: Begin with a few basic loose parts that can be used in a variety of ways. For example, start with a collection of natural materials such as stones, shells, and pinecones.
- Plan ahead: Consider what you have been observing about children's wonderings and actions, and decide what loose parts you can choose to support children's play. This will help you avoid getting too many items that won't be useful for now.

There are multiple ways to introduce loose parts to the children. You can simply place them in one or more of your centers (the construction and dramatic play areas are the two most obvious), letting children discover them on their own. A blog post at myteachingcupboard.com (n.d.) advises:

> Thoughtfully select the loose parts you offer and the way they are displayed. The way they are displayed will influence the way they are used. Displaying your loose parts in divided trays or individual bowls and baskets, which themselves create interest, will suggest the value of the loose parts resources. Children will be encouraged to take more care with these *special* items. They will also be more likely to use them respectfully and with thoughtful intent.

Another possibility for introducing loose parts is to use group time at the beginning of the day to let children know what to expect. Later, once the children are familiar with loose parts, you can use group time to introduce something new and perhaps unfamiliar. This gives you and the children a chance to discuss it, which will contribute to language development. Whatever choice you make, you'll want to talk with the children about cleanup protocols involving loose parts. Let them be involved in that discussion as well, so they feel some ownership of the protocols.

In previous chapters, I've encouraged you to make occasional changes to the materials in your centers to provide novelty. This holds true for loose parts as well. However, it's best to allow enough time for the children to *fully experience* the loose parts you've offered. We know how important repetition is for young children. But with loose parts in particular, we also want to give children ample opportunity to find multiple uses for them. That can't happen if they disappear too quickly.

As the children explore loose parts, your primary role is as an observer. When appropriate (that is, when you won't be interrupting a child's flow), you can scaffold the children's learning by asking such questions as, "How many spools do you have there?" Or, "What does that piece of fabric feel like to you?" You'll also want to note the children's strengths, where they may be having difficulties, and any developmental milestones they experience.

In addition to free play with loose parts, you can also offer guided play experiences, or "play invitations." For example, if the children have discovered a bird's nest and are showing curiosity about birds, you could provide a variety of loose parts that include feathers, twigs, cups of dirt, and something—perhaps marbles—to represent eggs. Haughey (n.d.-a) offers ideas for an outdoor play invitation involving spiderwebs. After asking the children to look for spiders outdoors, she divides the children into four groups, assigning each to an outdoor space of their own. She then gives a ball of thread to each child and invites the groups to create their own spiderweb. Ranheim (2020) offers such suggestions as asking the children to create patterns with a collection of rocks and cutting leaves in half and inviting the children to put the pieces back together.

Obviously, when it comes to loose parts, there's no end to the possibilities.

RECOMMENDED RESOURCES

- In addition to *Loose Parts: Inspiring Play in Young Children* (noted in References), Lisa Daly and Miriam Beloglovsky have written *Loose Parts 2: Inspiring Play With Infants and Toddlers*; *Loose Parts 3: Inspiring Culturally Sustainable Environments*; and *Loose Parts 4: Inspiring 21st Century Learning*. Daly has also written *Loose Parts in Action: The Essential How-To Guide*, and Beloglovsky has written *Loose Parts for Children With Diverse Abilities*.
- Within Sally Haughey's article "Loose Parts Play: A Guide for Early Educators," there are two links offering free downloads. One is for Wunderled's *Loose Parts Wish List* and the other for *Loose Parts: A Start Up Guide*. You can find the article with the links here: https://wunderled.com/blog/how-to-get-started-with-loose-parts/.
- Haughey has also written "23 Ways to Use Loose Parts Play for Academic Learning": https://wunderled.com/blog/23-ways-to-use-loose-parts-play-for-academic-learning/.
- Natural playscape designer and author Rusty Keeler has created a downloadable guide titled *Rusty's Outdoor Loose Parts List*. It covers the benefits of loose parts, how to manage loose parts,

and what loose parts to choose. It can be downloaded at https://rustykeeler.com/loosepartslistfd/.

> **PARTNERING WITH PARENTS**
>
> Parents want the best for their children, and, to them, that commonly means the latest and greatest in store-bought toys. A stroll through the toy aisle of a department store, with its bright colors and flashy packaging, or the marketing campaigns of toy companies, can be enough to turn almost any parent's head. Both make fantastic claims regarding the products' supposed educational value and fun. It's no wonder, then, that upon presenting these products to their children, parents are often perplexed to discover their child prefers the boxes they came in!
>
> You can help parents understand a child's preference for open-ended, multiple-use items over a toy that has only one predetermined use. Perhaps begin by asking parents if they've ever witnessed their child playing with a box instead of the toy or game that came in it. Have they ever seen their child become bored all too quickly with something they thought would excite them? If you can relate what you want to share about open-ended materials to their personal experiences, parents are more likely to have an "aha" moment.
>
> As I've suggested in previous chapters, you'll want to share information with parents via your emails or news updates. Let parents know, a little bit at a time, about the many values of loose parts play—and why open-ended materials are of greater benefit to their children than single-use toys. I would highly recommend you provide parents with a list of potential loose parts they can find and offer at home (see materials cited throughout this chapter). To involve them in their child's classroom experience, you also can ask them to donate loose parts. Parents are an excellent source for materials.
>
> You might also consider adding *Beautiful Stuff: Learning With Found Materials* to your lending library. Written specifically for parents by Cathy Weisman Topal and Lella Gandini, the book uses the real-life experiences of teachers and children to inspire ideas that can be tried at home. The ideas are appropriate for children ages 4 and up.

Conclusion

I once wrote that I shouldn't have to defend play for children any more than I should have to defend their eating, sleeping, or breathing. I stand by that statement. And I would add that neither should you have to defend play.

Unfortunately, a world in which none of us has to advocate for play is not yet the one in which we live. As much as it pains me to justify something nature intended for children—and that brings children such joy—I do it because I have no choice. If children are going to be denied something as essential and natural as play, I—and all of us who love them, who live and work with them—must do everything we can to right that wrong.

As Lisa Murphy (2016) has written

> The *proving* of the importance of play has already been done. We have years of research that document the many benefits of play as fostering and encouraging the intellectual, social, emotional, physical, language, and spiritual development of our children. In light of all this existing research, it would seem, then, that our job would be to apply this knowledge in schools and classrooms. Or so it would appear. For many educators, this is just simply not the case. Many educators find themselves in environments where, for whatever reason, it is still necessary for them to *prove* that play is very important. (p. 172)

Believe me, I know how incredibly frustrating this is. I also know that many early childhood educators find it difficult to imagine themselves as advocates, which means they find it difficult to imagine creating change. I never saw myself as an advocate. *Advocacy* is a scary word, conjuring images of protesting, standing before microphones at school board meetings, or testifying before Congress. But then someone suggested I write a book on advocacy for early childhood professionals, pointing out that I'd been speaking up for children throughout my career . . . and that made me an advocate!

As a keynote speaker and author, I had a platform from which to encourage change where I felt it was needed. But if you work with young children and parents, you have the best platform of all. Advocacy is just another word for *educate*—and educating is what you do. Throughout this book, I've recommended simple ways you can help parents understand the value of play. Perhaps, though, you feel this isn't enough to make a difference. But

I believe it's the single most important thing you can do to create change in our field. As I pointed out in the Introduction, the strength of parents' belief in early academics brought about the demise of many play-based programs. If we can help parents see that play is a *must* for their children, parents will help us turn things around!

When I speak about advocacy in early childhood education, I often use the example of a dripping faucet. Visualize the faucet's slow drip. One drip at a time may seem to be merely an annoyance. But if left unattended, all those little drips will eventually fill the sink and, in time, flood the room. Similarly, every time you help a parent—or a decision-maker—recognize that play is not separate from learning, you will have made a difference! Just as one drip at a time eventually changes a room and even a home, educating one parent or decision-maker at a time can change our profession and children's lives.

I hope you will use the information and suggestions in this book to give children more opportunity to play and to promote play's many benefits. Together we *can* make a difference.

References

Aguilar, E. (2018, February 6). The power of empathy. *Edutopia*. https://www.edutopia.org/article/power-empathy/

American Association for the Child's Right to Play. (n.d.) Promoting recess. https://ipausa.org/resources/recess/promoting-recess/

Anderer, J. (2023, March 17). Modern children deprived of independence, and it could be behind rise of early mental health problems. *Study Finds*. https://studyfinds.org/modern-children-independence-mental-health/

Anderssen, E. (2013, October 9). This school banned cartwheels, tag, balls, fun at recess. *The Globe and Mail*. https://www.theglobeandmail.com/life/the-hot-button/middle-school-bans-cartwheels-tag-all-sorts-of-balls-fun-at-recess/article14768645/

Anthony, M. (n.d.) Creative development in 3-5 year olds. *Scholastic*. https://www.scholastic.com/parents/family-life/creativity-and-critical-thinking/development-milestones/creative-development-3-5-year-olds.html

Bailey, E. (2023, May 15). Why childhood obesity rates are rising and what we can do. *Healthline*. https://www.healthline.com/health-news/why-childhood-obesity-rates-are-rising-and-what-we-can-do

Bassok, D., Latham, S., & Rorem, A. (2016). "Is kindergarten the new first grade?" *AERA Open 1*(4). https://doi.org/10.1177/2332858415616358.

Bisnath, J. (n.d.). Risky play—Essential for healthy child development. *Child Care Providers Resource Network*. https://ccprn.com/risky-play-essential-for-healthy-child-development/

Blackburn, P. (2023, July). Outsmart the wiggles. *Community Playthings*. https://www.communityplaythings.com/resources/articles/outsmart-the-wiggles

Blaschka, A. (2019, March 2). The number one soft skill employers seek—and five ways top leaders say to cultivate yours. *Forbes*. https://www.forbes.com/sites/amyblaschka/2019/02/28/the-number-one-soft-skill-employers-seek-and-five-ways-top-leaders-say-to-cultivate-yours/

Blinkoff, E., Fletcher, K., Wright, C., Espinoza, S., & Hirsh-Pasek, K. (2023, October 9). Tracking the winds of change on the American education policy landscape: The emergence of play-based learning legislation and its implications for the classroom. *Brookings*. https://www.brookings.edu/articles/tracking-the-winds-of-change-on-the-american-education-policy-landscape-the-emergence-of-play-based-learning-legislation-and-its-implications-for-the-classroom/

Brussoni, M. (2017). How to talk to parents about "risky play." *Child in the City*. https://www.childinthecity.org/2017/09/08/how-to-talk-to-parents-about-risky-play/

Brussoni, M., Givvons, R., Gray, C., Ishikawa, T., Sandseter, E.B.H., Bienenstock, A., Chabot, G., Fuselli, P., Herrington, S., Janssen, I., Pickett, W., Power, M., Stanger, N., Sampson, M., & Tremblay, M. S. (2015). What is the relationship between risky outdoor play and health in children? A systematic review. *International Journal of Environmental Research and Public Health*, *12*(6). https://www.mdpi.com/1660-4601/12/6/6423

Business Wire. (2018, September 20). *Survey finds today's children are spending 35% less time playing freely outside* [Press release]. https://www.businesswire.com/news/home/20180920005526/en/Survey-Finds-Today%E2%80%99s-Children-Are-Spending-35-Less-Time-Playing-Freely-Outside

Carlson, F. (n.d.) Touching children in the classroom: Why no-touch policies are harmful [Audio podcast]. https://www.bamradionetwork.com/track/touching-children-in-the-classroom-why-no-touch-policies-harmful/

Clark, L. (2012, November 7). The children being held back at school because their lazy lifestyles mean they can't stand on one leg. *Daily Mail*. https://www.dailymail.co.uk/health/article-2229567/The-children-held-school-lazy-lifestyles-mean-t-stand-leg.html

Clay, R. A. (2023, September 26). The many wondrous benefits of unstructured play. *American Psychological Association*. https://www.apa.org/topics/children/kids-unstructured-play-benefits

Covel, D. (2023, January 30). Is "stranger danger" still relevant to teach kids? *Healthnews*. https://healthnews.com/family-health/family-relations/is-stranger-danger-still-relevant-to-teach-kids/

Daly, L., & Beloglovsky, M. (2014). *Loose parts: Inspiring play in young children*. Redleaf Press.

Dodd, H. F., & Lester, K. J. (2021). Adventurous play as a mechanism for reducing risk of childhood anxiety: A conceptual model. *Clinical Child and Family Psychology Review*, *24*(1). https://www.ncbi.nlm.nih.gov/pmc/articles/PMC7880968

Eliot, G. (2003). *The mill on the floss*. Penguin Classics. (Original published in 1860)

ExRx.net. (n.d.). *Tag banned in schools across America: In midst of childhood obesity epidemic*. https://exrx.net/Questions/Tag

First Five Years. (2020, February 22). The benefits of nature play for children. *First Five Years*. https://www.firstfiveyears.org.au/early-learning/the-benefits-of-nature-play-for-children

Fox, H., & Worth, S. (2015, March). The learning in loose parts. *Community Playthings*. https://www.communityplaythings.com/resources/articles/the-learning-in-loose-parts

Fox, L. (2020). Some U.S. cities have banned a favorite winter pastime—snow sledding. *UPI*. https://www.upi.com/Top_News/US/2020/12/25/Some-US-cities-have-banned-a-favorite-winter-pastime-snow-sledding/3041608838714/

Franken, R. E. (2006). *Human motivation*. Cengage.

Gadzikowski, A. (2021). *Young architects at play: STEM activities for young children*. Redleaf Press.

Godwin, K. E., Almeda, M. A., Seltman, H., Kai, S., Skerbetz, M. D., Baker, R. S., & Fisher, A. V. (2016). Off-task behavior in elementary school children. *Learning and Instruction*, *44*, 128–43.

Gray, P. (2010, January 26). The decline of play and rise in children's mental disorders: There's a reason kids are more anxious and depressed than ever. *Psychology Today*. https://www.psychologytoday.com/intl/blog/freedom-learn/201001/the-decline-play-and-rise-in-childrens-mental-disorders

Gray, P. (2014, April 7). Risky play: Why children love and need it. *Psychology Today*. https://www.psychologytoday.com/us/blog/freedom-learn/201404/risky-play-why-children-love-it-and-need-it

Gray, P. (2022, September 16). Kids want to cooperate, but we make them compete. *Psychology Today*. https://www.psychologytoday.com/us/blog/freedom-learn/202209/kids-want-cooperate-we-make-them-compete

Hamilton, J. (2014, August 6). Scientists say child's play helps build a better brain. *NPR Ed*. https://www.npr.org/sections/ed/2014/08/06/336361277/scientists-say-childs-play-helps-build-a-better-brain

Hanscom, A. J. (2016). *Balanced and barefoot: How unrestricted outdoor play makes for strong, confident, and capable children*. New Harbinger Publications.

Hanscom, A. J. (2017, April). Risk-taking and child behaviour: Remove the bubble wrap. *Community Playthings*. https://www.communityplaythings.co.uk/learning-library/articles/remove-the-bubble-wrap

Harding, J. (2023). *The brain that loves to play: A visual guide to child development, play, and brain growth*. Routledge.

Hart, J. L., & Tannock, M. T. (2013, June). Young children's play fighting and use of war toys. *Encyclopedia on Early Childhood Development*. https://www.child-encyclopedia.com/play/according-experts/young-childrens-play-fighting-and-use-war-toys

Haughey, S. (n.d.-a). Exploring spider webs. *Wunderled*. https://wunderled.com/play-invitations/exploring-spider-webs/

Haughey, S. (n.d.-b). Loose parts play: A guide for early educators. *Wunderled*. https://wunderled.com/blog/how-to-get-started-with-loose-parts/

Herrity, J. (2023, July 31). 15 top qualities employers look for in job candidates. https://www.indeed.com/career-advice/finding-a-job/qualities-employers-want

Hintzen, K. (2015, July 2). The consequences of children spending less time outdoors. *Michigan State University Extension*. https://www.bluedynamo.msu.edu/news/the_consequences_of_children_spending_less_time_outdoors#:~:text=Access%20to%20green%20space%20has,obesity%20and%20Type%20II%20diabetes.

Hirsh-Pasek, K., & Golinkoff, R. (2003). *Einstein never used flashcards*. Rodale.

Huber, M. (2017). *Embracing rough-and-tumble play: Teaching with the body in mind*. Redleaf Press.

Indeed Editorial Team. (2022). 15 top qualities employers look for in job candidates. *Indeed*. https://www.indeed.com/career-advice/finding-a-job/qualities-employers-want

Ingraham, C. (2015, April 14). There's never been a safer time to be a kid in America. *Washington Post*: https://www.washingtonpost.com/news/wonk/wp/2015/04/14/theres-never-been-a-safer-time-to-be-a-kid-in-america/

IPA/USA (International Play Association USA Affiliate). (2019). *Promoting Recess*. IPA/USA. https://www.ipausa.org/recess_pages/promoting_recess.html.

Isbell, C. (2018, June). Hands at play: Developing fine motor skills for life. *Community Playthings*. https://www.communityplaythings.com/resources/articles/hands-at-play

Jackson, S. (2023, March 10). I quit my job as a teacher after 6 years to work in tech sales. I make $20,000 more, have greater flexibility in my day, and am so much happier now. *Business Insider*. https://www.businessinsider.com/why-i-quit-teaching-happier-make-more-money-2023-3

Jantz, J. (2022, August 8). What is rough and tumble play? An educator's guide. *Rasmussen University*. https://www.rasmussen.edu/degrees/education/blog/rough-and-tumble-play/

Jaques-Dalcroze, E. (1931). *Eurythmics, Art, and Education* (F. Rothwell, Trans.). Barnes.

Jargon, J. (2023, August 26). Screens, lack of sun are causing epidemic of myopia. *Wall Street Journal*. https://www.wsj.com/tech/personal-tech/our-eyes-really-are-getting-worse-heres-how-to-save-your-kids-vision-de16d592

Jarrett, O. S., & Maxwell, D. M. (2000). What research says about the need for recess. In Rhonda L. Clements (Ed.), *Elementary school recess: Selected readings, games, and activities for teachers and parents* (pp. 12–23). American Press.

Jensen, E. (2000). *Learning with the body in mind: The scientific basis for energizers, movement, play, games, and physical education*. Brain Store.

Jensen, E. (2001). *Arts with the brain in mind*. ASCD.

Jones, D. (2017, December 4). The teacher's role during play. *Defending the Early Years*. https://dey.org/the-teachers-role-during-play/

Jones, G., Carlsson-Paige, N., & Guernsey, L. (n.d.) War, gun, and super-hero play: Good or bad? [Audio podcast]. BRN. https://www.bamradionetwork.com/track/war-guns-and-super-hero-play-good-or-bad/

Jones, S. (2023, September 14). Why do we play? Rats can teach us how it improves mental health. *The Washington Post*. https://www.washingtonpost.com/wellness/2023/09/14/play-mental-health-brain-strategies/

Kamenetz, A. (2015, May 14). Vindication for fidgeters: Movement may help students with ADHD concentrate. *NPR Ed*. https://www.npr.org/sections/ed/2015/05/14/404959284/fidgeting-may-help-concentration-for-students-with-adhd

Kamenetz, A. (2018, April 29). What "A Nation at Risk" got wrong, and right, about U.S. schools. *NPR Ed*. https://www.npr.org/sections/ed/2018/04/29/604986823/what-a-nation-at-risk-got-wrong-and-right-about-u-s-schools

Keeler, R. (2020). *Adventures in risky play: What is your yes?* Dimensions Educational Research Foundation.

Kellert, S. R. (2002). Experiencing nature: Affective, cognitive, and evaluative development in children. In P. H. Kahn, Jr., & S. R. Kellert (Eds.), *Children and nature: Psychological, sociocultural, and evolutionary investigations* (pp. 117–151). Massachusetts Institute of Technology.

Kelley, R., & Kelley, B. (2017). Just wrestle: How we evolved through rough and tumble play. *Journal of Evolution and Health*, *2*(3). https://escholarship.org/content/qt6j76b25h/qt6j76b25h.pdf

Kemple, K. (2017). *Planning for play: Strategies for guiding preschool learning*. Gryphon House.

Kennedy, R. (2018, January 15). Children spend half the time playing outside in comparison to their parents. *Child in the City*. https://www.childinthecity.org

/2018/01/15/children-spend-half-the-time-playing-outside-in-comparison-to-their-parents/

Khomais, S., Al-Khalidi, N., & Alotaibi, D. (2019). Dramatic play in relation to self-regulation in preschool age. *Contemporary Issues in Education Research (CIER), 12*(4), 103–112. https://doi.org/10.19030/cier.v12i4.10323

Kohn, A. (1992). *No contest: The case against competition* (Revised ed.). Houghton Mifflin.

Kohn, A. (2007). *The homework myth: Why our kids get too much of a bad thing.* Da Capo Lifelong Books.

Korbey, H. (2012, February 22). Should preschoolers have homework? *The New York Times.* https://archive.nytimes.com/parenting.blogs.nytimes.com/2012/02/22/should-preschoolers-have-homework/

Kristof, N. D. (1998, April 12). Correspondence/uncompetitive in Tokyo; in Japan, nice guys (and girls) finish together. *The New York Times.* https://www.nytimes.com/1998/04/12/weekinreview/correspondence-uncompetitive-tokyo-japan-nice-guys-girls-finish-together.html

Kuo, M., Barnes, M., & Jordan, C. (2019). Do experiences with nature promote learning? Converging evidence of a cause-and-effect relationship. *Frontiers in Psychology, 10*, 305. https://doi.org/10.3389/fpsyg.2019.00305.

Levin, D. E. (2003). Beyond banning war and superhero play: Meeting children's needs in violent times. *Young Children, 58*(3), 60–63. https://fairplayforkids.org/wp-content/uploads/archive/levin_warplay.pdf

Lingham, G., Mackey, D. A., Lucas, R., & Yazar, S. (2020). How does spending time outdoors protect against myopia? A review. *British Journal of Ophthalmology, 104*, 593–599. https://bjo.bmj.com/content/104/5/593

Livshits, H. (2019). Sociodramatic pretend play: A vehicle to emotional self-regulation, language learning and school success. *The Hanen Centre.* https://www.hanen.org/SiteAssets/Articles---Printer-Friendly/Research-in-your-Daily-Work/Sociodramatic-Pretend-Play-PF.aspx

Louv, R. (2005). *Last child in the woods: Saving our children from nature-deficit disorder.* Algonquin Books.

Lyons, S. (2022). *Cooperative games in education: Building community without competition, pre-K–12.* Teachers College Press.

MacDonald, S. (2020). *Block play: The complete guide to learning and playing with blocks.* Gryphon House.

Mader, J. (2022, March 22). Kids can learn more from guided play than from direct instruction, report finds. *The Hechinger Report.* https://hechingerreport.org/kids-can-learn-more-from-guided-play-than-from-direct-instruction-report-finds/

Mader, J. (2023, June 29). "Guided play" benefits kids—but what does that look like for parents? *The Hechinger Report.* https://hechingerreport.org/guided-play-benefits-kids-but-what-does-that-look-like-for-parents/

McBride, N. A. (2011). Child safety is more than a slogan: "Stranger-danger" warnings not effective at keeping kids safer. *National Center for Missing and Exploited Children.* https://ojjdp.ojp.gov/sites/g/files/xyckuh176/files/pubs/252024.pdf

Mental Health Foundation. (n.d.). Nature: How connecting with nature benefits our mental health. https://www.mentalhealth.org.uk/our-work/research/nature-how-connecting-nature-benefits-our-mental-health

Morrongiello, B. A., & Dawber, T. (1999). Parental influences on toddlers' injury—risk behaviors: Are sons and daughters socialized differently? *Journal of Applied Developmental Psychology, 20*(2), 227–251.

Murphy, L. (2016). *Lisa Murphy on play: The foundation of children's learning.* Redleaf Press.

My Teaching Cupboard. (n.d.). Loose parts play. https://www.myteachingcupboard.com/blog/loose-parts-play

Nagel, M. (2019, March 18). Bringing up girls: Biology and behaviour. *First Five Years.* https://www.firstfiveyears.org.au/child-development/bringing-up-girls-biology-and-behaviour

National Council of Youth Sports. (n.d.). Keep youth in the game. https://ncys.org/safety/keep-youth-in-the-game/

National Institute for Play. (n.d.). Why we play. https://www.nifplay.org/what-is-play/biological-drive-to-play/

Oliver, S. J., & Klugman, E. (2005). Play and the outdoors: What's new under the sun? *Exchange, 7.*

O'Neal, E. E., Plumert, J. M. & Peterson, C. (2016). Parent-child injury prevention conversations following a trip to the emergency department. *Journal of Pediatric Psychology, 41*(2), 256–264.

Orlick, T. (2006). *The cooperative sports and games book: Joyful activities for everyone* (2nd ed.). Human Kinetics.

Patte, M. (n.d.). The decline of unstructured play. *The Genius of Play.* https://www.thegeniusofplay.org/genius/expert-advice/articles/the-decline-of-unstructured-play.aspx

Paul, A. M. (2021). *The extended mind: The power of thinking outside the brain.* Houghton Mifflin Harcourt.

Paul, C. (2016, February 20). Why do we teach girls that it's cute to be scared? *The New York Times.* https://www.nytimes.com/2016/02/21/opinion/sunday/why-do-we-teach-girls-that-its-cute-to-be-scared.html

Pica, R. (2013). *Experiences in movement and music* (5th ed.). Wadsworth.

Pica, R. (2023). *Spark a revolution in early education: Speaking up for ourselves and the children.* Redleaf Press.

Ranheim, D. (2020, August). Math play with loose parts. *Community Playthings.* https://www.communityplaythings.com/resources/articles/math-play-with-loose-parts

Rantala, T., & Määttä, K. (2012). Ten theses of the joy of learning at primary schools. *Early Child Development and Care, 182*(1), 87–105. https://psycnet.apa.org/doi/10.1080/03004430.2010.545124

Rivkin, M. S., & Schein, D. (2014). *The great outdoors: Advocating for natural spaces for young children* (Rev. ed.). National Association for the Education of Young Children.

Rochman, B. (2012, December 31). Yay for recess: Pediatricians say it's as important as math or reading. *Time.* https://healthland.time.com/2012/12/31/yay-for-recess-pediatricians-say-its-as-important-as-math-or-reading/

Rubin, K., Fein, G., & Vandenberg, B. (1983). Play. In E. Hetherington (Ed.) & P. Mussen (Series Ed.,), *Handbook of child psychology: Vol. 4. Socialization, personality, and social development* (pp. 693–774). Wiley.

Sääkslahti, A., Howells, K., & DeMartalaer, K. (2021). Children's rough-and-tumble play in a supportive early childhood education and care environment.

International Journal of Environmental Research and Public Health, 18(19): 10469. https://www.ncbi.nlm.nih.gov/pmc/articles/PMC8507902/

Sahlberg, P., & Doyle, W. (2019). *Let the children play: How more play will save our schools and help children thrive.* Oxford University Press.

Salinas-Gonzalez, I., Arreguin, M. G., & Alanis, I. (2018). Supporting language: Culturally rich dramatic play. *Teaching Young Children, 11*(2). https://www.naeyc.org/resources/pubs/tyc/dec2017/supporting-language-culturally-rich-dramatic-play

Sampson, S. (2016). *How to raise a wild child: The art and science of falling in love with nature.* Mariner Books.

Sandseter, E.B.H. (2007). Categorizing risky play—how can we identify risk-taking in children's play? *European Early Childhood Education Research Journal, 15*(2), 237–252.

Science Daily. (2015, September 16). Immune system may be pathway between immune system and good health. https://www.sciencedaily.com/releases/2015/09/150916162120.htm

Skenazy, L. (2017, September 20). Canadian school bans cartwheels, because we can't be too careful. *Reason.* https://reason.com/2017/09/20/canadian-school-bans-cartwheeling-becaus/

Skenazy, L. (2023, August 26). Playground sign outlaws "loitering at slide entry or exit." *Reason.* https://reason.com/2023/08/26/playground-sign-outlaws-loitering-at-slide-entry-or-exit/

Skylar, H. (2017, January 26). Is a competitive nature learned or innate? *Orange County Register.* https://www.ocregister.com/2017/01/26/is-a-competitive-nature-learned-or-innate-2/

Sole-Smith, V. (2020). Should parents be concerned about violent play? *Parents.* https://www.parents.com/kids/development/should-parents-be-concerned-about-violent-play/

Storli, R. (2021). Children's rough-and-tumble play in a supportive early childhood education and care environment. *International Journal of Environmental Research and Public Health, 18*(19), 10469. https://www.ncbi.nlm.nih.gov/pmc/articles/PMC8507902

Storli, R., & Sandseter, E.B.H. (2015). Preschool teachers' perceptions of children's rough-and-tumble play (R&T) in indoor and outdoor environments. *Early Child Development and Care, 185*(11–12), 1995–2009. https://doi.org/10.1080/03004430.2015.1028394

Strauss, V. (2014, October 7). The right—and surprisingly wrong—ways to get kids to sit still in class. *Washington Post.* https://www.washingtonpost.com/news/answer-sheet/wp/2014/10/07/the-right-and-surprisingly-wrong-ways-to-get-kids-to-sit-still-in-class/

Tate Sullivan, E. (2021, February 9). The pandemic has compounded the turnover problem in early childhood education. *EdSurge.* https://www.edsurge.com/news/2021-02-09-the-pandemic-has-compounded-the-turnover-problem-in-early-childhood-education

University of Cambridge. (2022, January 12). Learning through "guided play" can be as effective as adult-led instruction. https://www.cam.ac.uk/research/news/learning-through-guided-play-can-be-as-effective-as-adult-led-instruction

Vines. P. (2012, August 29). Banning cartwheels: school litigation fears are unfounded. *The Conversation.* https://theconversation.com/banning-cartwheels-school-litigation-fears-are-unfounded-9140

Wang, M. L., & Gago, C. M. (2024). Shifts in child health behaviors and obesity after COVID-19. *JAMA Pediatrics, 178*(5), 427–428. doi:10.1001/jamapediatrics.2024.0027

Wardle, F. (2000). *Supporting constructive play in the wild.* Exchange Press. https://www.exchangepress.com/article/supporting-constructive-play-in-the-wild/5013326/

Weaver, M. (2018, October 30). Medical students raised on screens lack skills for surgery. *The Guardian.* https://www.theguardian.com/society/2018/oct/30/medical-students-raised-on-screens-lack-skills-for-surgery

Weisberg, D. S., & Zoss, J. M. (2018, February). How guided play promotes early childhood learning. *Encyclopedia on Early Childhood Development.* https://www.child-encyclopedia.com/play-based-learning/according-experts/how-guided-play-promotes-early-childhood-learning

Weisberg, D. S., Hirsh-Pasek, K., Golinkoff, R. M., Kittredge, A. K., & Klahr, D. (2016). Guided play: Principles and practices. *Current Directions in Psychological Science, 25*(3), 177–182.

Willis, J. (2007, June 1). The neuroscience of joyful education. ASCD: https://www.ascd.org/el/articles/the-neuroscience-of-joyful-education

Willis, J. (2014, July 18). The neuroscience behind stress and learning. *Edutopia.* https://www.edutopia.org/blog/neuroscience-behind-stress-and-learning-judy-willis

Index

Acre, Holly, 3
Active for Life, 12
Active learning, guided play as, 14
Aguilar, E., 71
Alanis, I., 71, 74
Al-Khalidi, N., 72
Alotaibi, D., 72
Alphabet Shapes (game), 18–19
Amag! magazine, 87
American Academy of Pediatrics (AAP), 11, 31, 33
American Association for the Child's Right to Play, 30
American Heart Association, 23
Anderer, J., 7
Anderssen, E., 47
Animals
   dramatic play and, 70, 75
   free play of, 11
   nature play and, 44
AnjiPlay, 52
Anthony, M., 70
Anxiety in children
   decline of play and, 2
   lack of free play and, 7
   nature play and, 41
   parental overprotectiveness and, 51
   risky play and, 49, 51
Arreguin, M. G., 71, 74
Art concepts
   guided play and, 17
   nature play and, 40–41, 44
Attention deficits, nature play and, 41

Bailey, E., 22
Balanced and Barefoot (Hanscom), 45
Balloon Volley (game), 80

Barefoot play, 42, 45
Barnes, M., 41
Bassok, D., 62
Beanbag Toss (game), 81
Beautiful Stuff (Topal & Gandini), 94
Beloglovsky, Miriam, 89, 93
Big body play, 22–29. *See also* Outdoor play; Rough-and-tumble play
   amount of activity needed, 23, 24–25
   benefits of, 22, 23, 24–25, 29, 77
   child lack of, 22–24
   construction play and, 85
   educator role in, 25–28
   fear/safety concerns and, 23, 47, 79
   fine motor skills and, 77, 79
   games in, 26–28
   gross motor skill development and, 23, 26, 77, 79, 85
   health-related fitness factors and, 24, 32
   nature of, 23, 25–26
   parents and, 28–29
   playgrounds and, 23, 26, 29, 30, 39, 46, 47, 52
   putting theory into practice, 25–28
   recommended resources, 28–29
Big Body Play (Carlson), 28
Bisnath, J., 49–50
Blackburn, Preston, 25
Blaschka, A., 7
Blast Off (game), in guided play, 15
Blinkoff, E., 4
Blob Tag (game), 27, 58
Block play, 5, 7, 9, 84–85, 86, 87–88
Bohart, Holly, 20

Boredom, free play and, 10–11
Bos, Bev, 5
Bottle Bowling (game), 36
Brain development. *See* Cognitive development
The Brain That Loves to Play (Harding), 8
British Journal of Ophthalmology, 32
BRN, 52, 56, 59, 74–75
Brown, Stuart, 55
Brussoni, Mariana, 48–53
Bubble Chase (game), 27
Business Wire, 30
Byrne, Elizabeth, 16

Carlson, Frances, 28, 56, 59
Carlsson-Paige, Nancy, 10, 54, 74, 75
Cartwheels, 23, 46, 47, 48
Cat and Mouse (game), 58
Chiffon scarves, 80, 90
Child development
  cognitive. *See* Cognitive development
  communication skills. *See* Communication skills
  emergent literacy. *See* Emergent literacy
  fine motor skills and, 76, 77–78, 85
  gross motor skills and, 23, 26, 77, 79, 85
  sensory. *See* Sensory development
  social-emotional. *See* Social-emotional development
  social skills. *See* Social skills
Child Mind Institute, 45
Children and Nature Network, 44
China, AnjiPlay philosophy of early education, 52
Clark, L., 25
Clay, R. A., 33
The Coddling of the American Mind (Lukianoff & Haidt), 52
Cognitive development
  big body play and, 22, 25, 26
  free play and, 8, 12
  guided play and, 16
  outdoor play and, 32–33

Collaboration
  cooperative play and, 63–65
  free play and, 7, 12
  importance in the workplace, 63
  loose parts play and, 91
  outdoor play and, 32
Communication skills
  construction play and, 86
  cooperative play and, 66, 86
  outdoor play and, 32
  rough-and-tumble play and, 55
Compassion, dramatic play and, 71
Competition, cooperative play vs., 61–65
Conflict resolution, free play and, 7
Connelly, Gail, 37
Construction play, 84–88. *See also* Loose parts play
  benefits of, 84–86
  block play in, 5, 7, 9, 84–85, 86, 87–88
  constructive play (Piaget) and, 84
  creativity and, 85, 87, 89–90
  educator role in, 86–87
  hands in, 85
  materials in, 84–87
  nature of, 84
  parents and, 88
  recommended resources, 87–88
Cook, Shana, 20
Cooperative Musical Chairs (game), 65–66
Cooperative play, 61–69
  benefits of, 63–65, 69
  competition vs., 61–65
  construction play and, 86
  educator role in, 65–68
  games in, 63, 65–69
  loose parts play and, 91
  outdoor play and, 32
  parents and, 69
  putting theory into practice, 65–68
  recommended resources, 69
Counting Fingers (game), 80
Covel, D., 31
Crawling, 23, 25, 26, 76, 79
Creative Block Play (Hansel), 88

Creativity. *See also* Imagination
 construction play and, 85, 87, 89–90
 defined, 71
 dramatic play and, 70–72, 74, 89–90
 free play and, 7–10, 12
 guided play and, 16
 importance in the workplace, 7
 loose parts play and, 89–90, 92
 outdoor play and, 32
Creatures in the Clouds (game), 36, 43
Creeping, 23, 26, 79

Daly, Lisa, 89, 93
Dawber, T., 47
Decision-making skills
 construction play and, 87
 guided play and, 15
 outdoor play and, 32
 in risky play, 49, 53
 risky play and, 49
Defending the Early Years, 9
Del Rio, Sara, 11
Depression in children
 decline of play and, 2
 lack of free play and, 7
 nature play and, 41
Direct instruction, 10, 15–16
Dodd, H. F., 49, 53
Doyle, William, 10, 29, 33, 34, 61
Dramatic play, 70–75. *See also* Loose parts play
 animals and, 70, 75
 benefits of, 70, 71–72, 73
 creativity and, 70–72, 74, 89–90
 educator role in, 73–74
 fear/safety concerns and, 72–73, 74–75
 gun play, 54, 59, 72–73, 74–75
 materials and, 73–74, 87
 nature of, 70
 parents and, 75
 putting theory into practice, 73–74
 recommended resources, 74–75
 safety and, 72–73, 74–75
 superhero play, 9, 59, 72–73, 74–75
 war play, 54, 59, 72–73, 74–75

Drive (Pink), 10
Dyment, Janet, 39

Early childhood education (ECE)
 ages for, 4
 burnout of educators in, 2–3
 competitive pressures in, 61–65
 direct instruction in, 10, 15–16
 early learning/play centers in, 8, 9, 14, 17, 65, 70, 76, 86, 92
 homework in, 2, 30
 lack of recess, 30
 low wages in, 3
 productivity/achievement focus in, 1–4
Early learning/play centers, 8, 9, 14, 17, 65, 70, 76, 86, 92
Edutopia, 75
Einstein Never Used Flashcards (Hirsh-Pasek & Golinkoff), 13
Elbow Tag (game), 58–59
Electronic technology. *See* Screen time
Eliot, George, 42
Emergent literacy
 construction play and, 86
 dramatic play and, 71, 74
 fine motor play and writing, 76–78, 79–80, 81, 82, 83
 guided play and, 14–15, 17, 18–20
 loose parts play and, 90
Empathy, dramatic play and, 71, 72
The Encyclopedia on Early Childhood Development (Sole-Smith), 72
Environment
 nature play and, 41, 42
 outdoor play and, 32–33
Espinoza, S., 4
Essential Touch (Carlson), 59
Executive-function skills
 free play and, 11–12
 guided play and, 15–16
 risky play and, 49–50
 rough-and-tumble play and, 55
Ex.Rx.net, 23
Extrinsic (passive) learning, guided play vs., 14
Eye-hand coordination, 36, 78–81, 85

Fantasy play. *See* Dramatic play
Fear/safety concerns
  big body play and, 23, 47, 79
  culture of fear and, 2
  dramatic play and, 72–73, 74–75
  fine motor play and, 79
  loose parts play and, 91
  nature play and, 39
  outdoor play and, 2, 30–31, 47
  risks vs. hazards and, 47
  risky play and, 46–48
  rough-and-tumble play and, 56–57, 59–60
Fein, G., 84
Fine motor play, 76–83. *See also* Loose parts play
  benefits of, 76, 78–79
  construction play and, 85
  educator role in, 79–82
  eye-hand coordination and, 36, 78–81
  fear/safety concerns and, 79
  games in, 80–82
  hands of children and, 76, 77–81, 82
  nature of fine motor development, 76, 77–78, 85
  parents and, 76, 83
  putting theory into practice, 79–82
  recommended resources, 82–83
  writing and fine motor skills, 76–83
Finland
  research on joy, 6
  research on recess, 33
Fiore, Lisa, 56
First Five Years, 39
Fletcher, K., 4
Florida Atlantic University, 7
Follow the Leader (game), in outdoor play, 35
Forbes, 7
Fox, H., 89
Fox, L., 47
Franken, R. E., 71
Free play, 5–12. *See also* Loose parts play; Nature play
  benefits of, 5–8, 10–12
  educator role in, 8–9
  games vs., 5
  inability to play and, 10–12
  joy in, 5–7
  nature of, 5
  open-ended materials in, 8–9
  parents and, 10–11
  putting theory into practice, 8–9
  recommended resources, 10–12
  space and, 8, 9
  structured play vs., 9
  time and, 8, 9
Free-Range Kids (Skenazy), 37, 38, 52
Free-Range Kids website, 37, 48, 52
Free time, impact of too little, 1–2
Freud, Sigmund, 63

Gadzikowski, Ann, 84–87
Gago, C. M., 53
Games
  See My Hands, 80–81
  Alphabet Shapes, 18–19
  Balloon Volley, 80
  Beanbag Toss, 81
  in big body play, 26–28
  Blob Tag, 27, 58
  Bottle Bowling, 36
  Bubble Chase, 27
  Cat and Mouse, 58
  Cooperative Musical Chairs, 65–66
  in cooperative play, 63, 65–69
  Counting Fingers, 80
  Creatures in the Clouds, 36, 43
  Elbow Tag, 58–59
  in fine motor play, 80–82
  Follow the Leader, 35
  free play vs., 5
  Going on a Treasure Hunt, 44
  Group Balance, 67
  in guided play, 13, 14–15, 17–20, 43
  Hoop Jump, 28
  Hopscotch, 28
  It Takes Two, 19
  Lightning and Thunder, 68
  A Listening Walk, 35, 43
  Making Waves, 82
  Mirror Game, 67
  Mix It Up, 44
  Musical Chairs, 63, 65, 66

Musical Magical Hoops, 19
My Hands Can, 81
 in nature play, 43–44
 Nature's Art, 44
 Nature's Music, 43
 in outdoor play, 35–36
 Pass a Face, 66
 Pass a Movement, 67
 "Pop Goes the Weasel," 27
 Rabbits and 'Roos, 27
 Reverse Tag, 59
 Ring Toss, 36
 Rotate It, 81–82
 in rough-and-tumble play, 58–59
 Shadow Game, 68
 Shadow Tag, 35, 58
 Shrinking Room, 17–18
 Simon Says, 19–20
 Statues, 13, 14–15, 35
 Switcheroo, 68
 This Is My Friend, 67
 Touch It, 26–27, 43
 Turtle Tag, 58
 Writing in Space, 82
Gandini, Lelia, 94
Gender
 risky play and, 47, 48, 51
 rough-and-tumble play and, 55–58, 59, 60
Global Recess Alliance, 37
Godwin, Karrie, 33
Going on a Treasure Hunt (game), 44
Golinkoff, R., 13, 90
Gray, Peter, 2, 51, 53, 63
Great Games for Young Children (Pica), 69
The Great Outdoors (Rivkin & Schein), 41–42
Groos, Carl, 54
Gross motor play. *See* Big body play
Group Balance (game), 67
Grove, Jim, 12
Guernsey, L., 54, 74
Guided play, 13–21
 benefits of, 13–16, 20–21
 direct instruction vs., 16
 in dramatic play, 74

 educator role in, 16–20
 games in, 13, 14–15, 17–20, 43
 learning goals and, 13–14, 16–17, 20–21
 nature of, 13–15
 in nature play, 43
 parents and, 20–21
 putting theory into practice, 16–20
 recommended resources, 20–21
Gun play, 54, 59, 72–73, 74–75

Haidt, Jonathan, 52
Hamilton, J., 32
Hands of children
 eye-hand coordination and, 36, 78–81, 85
 fine motor play and, 76, 77–81, 82
Hannaford, Carla, 28
Hanscom, Angela J., 24–25, 40, 42, 45, 49, 83
Hansel, Rosanne, 88
Harding, Jacqueline, 8
Harlow, Harry, 54
Hart, J. I., 72, 73
Haughey, Sally, 92, 93
Hautala, Bob, 62
Hintzen, K., 30
Hirsh-Pasek, Kathy, 4, 13, 16, 20, 90
Home environment
 big body play and, 29
 free play and, 8
 guided play and, 20–21
 loose parts play and, 94
Homework, 2, 30
Hoop Jump (game), 28
Hopscotch (game), 28
How to Raise a Wild Child (Sampson), 41
Huber, Mike, 55, 56–57, 59–60

Imagination. *See also* Creativity
 construction play and, 85, 87
 dramatic play and, 74
 free play and, 7–10
 nature play and, 43
 superhero play and, 9, 59, 72–73, 74–75

Immune system, nature play and, 41
Indeed Editorial Team, 63
Independence
  free play and, 7
  guided play and, 13
  risky play and, 48–49, 50–51, 52–53
  rough-and-tumble play and, 57
Ingraham, C., 31, 38
Instructional time, recess and, 33
International Journal of Environmental Research and Public Health, 54–55
International Myopia Institute, 38
Intrinsic (active) learning, guided play as, 14
Intrinsic motivation, 6–7
IPA/USA (International Play Association USA Affiliate), 37
Isbell, Christy, 78, 79, 80, 82–83
It Takes Two (game), 19

Jackson, S., 3
Jantz, J., 54
Jaques-Dalcroze, Emile, 6
Jargon, J., 32
Jarrett, Olga S., 33
Jensen, Eric, 14, 33
Jones, Denisha, 9
Jones, Gerard, 54, 74, 75
Jones, S., 54, 55
Jordan, C., 41
Joy, 5–7

Kahn, P. H., Jr., 41
Kamenetz, A., 61
Katch, Jane, 75
Keeler, Rusty, 47, 51, 52, 93–94
Kellert, Stephen R., 41
Kelley, B., 54
Kelley, R., 54
Kemple, K., 70, 72, 73–74
Kennedy, R., 30
Khomais, S., 72
Killing Monsters (Jones), 75
Klugman, Edgar, 42–43
Kneebone, Roger, 76
Kohn, Alfie, 2, 63–64, 69
Korbey, H., 30

Kristof, Nicholas D., 63
Kuo, Ming, 41

Language development. *See* Emergent literacy
Large motor play. *See* Big body play
Last Child in the Woods (Louv), 31, 40
Latham, S., 62
Learning Across the Curriculum (Pica), 20
LEGO Foundation, 20–21
Legos, 84, 87
Lesley University, 56
Lester, K. J., 49, 53
Lethargy, 24
Let the Children Play (Sahlberg & Doyle), 10, 29, 34
Levin, Diane, 73, 75
Lightning and Thunder (game), 68
LiiNK, 37
Lingham, G., 32
A Listening Walk (game), 35, 43
Literacy development. *See* Emergent literacy
Livshits, H., 72
Locomotor skills, 26
Loose parts play, 89–94
  benefits of, 89–91
  educator role in, 91–93
  nature of, 89
  open-ended vs. single-use materials and, 89–90, 94
  parents and, 94
  putting theory into practice, 91–93
  recommended resources, 93–94
Louv, Richard, 31, 40, 42
Lucas, R., 32
Lukianoff, Greg, 52
Luvmour, Ba, 69
Luvmour, Josette, 69
Lyons, Suzanne, 61, 64, 69

Määttä, K., 6
MacDonald, Sharon, 86, 88
Mackey, D. A., 32

Mader, J., 16, 20–21
Making Waves (game), 82
Manipulatives, in guided play, 16, 17
Masterson, Marie, 20
Materials. *See also* Construction play; Loose parts play
　changes in, for novelty, 73, 92
　in construction play, 84–87
　dramatic play and, 73–74, 87
　fine motor play and, 78–79, 80
　free play and, 8–9
　manipulatives in guided play, 16, 17
Math concepts
　construction play and, 85
　direct instruction and, 16
　guided play and, 14, 16, 17
　loose parts play and, 91
　outdoor play and, 32
Maxwell, Darlene M., 33
McBride, N. A., 2
Mead, Margaret, 63
Mental Health Foundation, 41
Mercer, Alfred, 6
Michigan State University, research on outdoor play, 30
Mighty Fine Motor Fun (Isbell), 82
Mirror Game, 67
Mix It Up (game), 44
Mood disorders, nature play and, 41
Morgan, Amanda, 83
Morrongiello, B. A., 47
Moving & Learning Series (Pica), 28
Multop, Gail, 52
Murphy, Lisa, 95
Murray, Robert, 33
Musical Chairs (game), 63, 65, 66
Musical Magical Hoops (game), 19
Music concepts
　cooperative play and, 63, 65, 66
　direct instruction and, 16
　free play and, 6
　guided play and, 17, 19
My Hands Can (game), 81
Myopia (nearsightedness), outdoor play and, 32, 38
Myteachingcupboard.com, 92

Nagel, M., 54, 55, 60
National Association for the Education of Young Children (NAEYC), 20, 44, 75
National Association of Elementary School Principals, 37
National Center for Missing and Exploited Children, 2, 31
National Council of Youth Sports, 53
National Institute for Play, 1, 55
National Wildlife Foundation, 44
"A Nation at Risk," 61
Nature play, 39–45. *See also* Free play; Loose parts play
　animals and, 44
　benefits of, 39, 40–42
　educator role in, 42–44
　fear/safety concerns and, 39
　games in, 43–44
　going barefoot, 42, 45
　guided play in, 43
　nature of, 39
　parents and, 45
　putting theory into practice, 42–44
　recommendations for, 42–43
　recommended resources, 44–45
Nature Play (film), 44, 45
Nature's Art (game), 44
Nature's Music (game), 43
Nearsightedness (myopia), outdoor play and, 32, 38
Negotiation
　dramatic play and, 72
　free play and, 7
　loose parts play and, 91
New Zealand, research on recess, 49
Nicholson, Simon, 89–90
No Child Left Behind, 61–62
No Contest (Kohn), 69
Nonlocomotor skills, 26

Obesity, 8, 22–24
Obstacle courses, 14, 26, 35
Oliver, Susan J., 42–43
O'Neal, E. E., 47
Open Educational Resources (OER), 87
Orlick, Terry, 67, 69

Outdoor play, 30–38. *See also* Big body play; Loose parts play; Rough-and-tumble play
  amount of activity needed, 30, 33
  benefits of, 30, 31–34, 37–38
  body-management skills in, 34
  educator role in, 34–36
  examples of, 34–35
  fear/safety concerns and, 2, 30–31, 47
  games in, 35–36
  health-related fitness factors and, 24, 32
  myopia (nearsightedness) and, 32, 38
  obstacle courses, 14, 26, 35
  parachute play, 26, 34, 64, 81–82
  parents and, 2, 30–31, 33, 37–38
  playgrounds and, 23, 26, 29, 30, 39, 46, 47, 52, 93–94
  putting theory into practice, 34–36
  recess/breaks in schools and, 30, 31, 33–34, 37–38, 49
  recommendations for, 42–43
  recommended resources, 37–38
Overprotectiveness, 47, 51, 52
Overscheduling, 2, 23, 30, 39

Parachute play, 26, 34, 64, 81–82
Parent and Advocates Guide, 52
Parents. *See also* Home environment
  advocacy for play and, 4, 95–96
  big body play and, 28–29
  construction play and, 88
  cooperative play and, 69
  dramatic play and, 75
  fear/safety concerns and, 2, 30–31, 39, 47
  fine motor play and, 76, 83
  free play and, 10–11
  guided play and, 20–21
  lending library for, 75, 88, 94
  loose parts play and, 94
  misinformation and, 3–4
  nature play and, 45
  outdoor play and, 2, 30–31, 33, 37–38
  overprotective, 47, 51, 52
  overscheduling and, 2, 23, 30, 39
  parent-teacher conferences/gatherings, 10, 11, 38
  risky play and, 46–48, 50–51, 52–53
  rough-and-tumble play and, 56–57, 59–60
  sample letter to, 88
Pass a Face (game), 66
Pass a Movement (game), 67
Patte, Michael, 7–9
Paul, Annie Murphy, 33
Paul, C., 47
Perceptual skills, nature play and, 40
Persistence/perseverance, 48, 64, 85, 87, 91
Perspective-taking
  big body play and, 25
  free play and, 7
Peterson, C., 47
Physical development. *See* Outdoor play; Risky play; Rough-and-tumble play
Piaget, Jean, 84
Pica, Rae, 4, 20, 24, 28, 69
Pink, Daniel, 10
Play
  advocacy for, 3–4, 95–96
  amount of activity needed, 23, 24–25, 30, 33
  defining, 5
  direct instruction vs., 10, 15–16
  games and. *See* Games
  health-related fitness factors and, 24, 32, 56
  impact of too little, 1–2, 3–4
  overlap among types of play, 3
  problems of young children with, 1–2, 3–4
  productivity/achievement focus vs., 1–4
  sports vs., 2, 5
Play centers/early learning centers, 8, 9, 14, 17, 65, 70, 76, 86, 92
Playgrounds, 23, 26, 29, 30, 39, 46, 47, 52, 93–94
Play of Animals (Groos), 54
Play of Man (Groos), 54

Playscape design, 93–94
Plumert, J. M., 47
"Pop Goes the Weasel" (game), 27
Posture, 24
Pretend play. *See* Dramatic play
Problem-solving skills
    construction play and, 85, 87
    cooperative play and, 65–66
    dramatic play and, 71
    free play and, 7, 12
    guided play and, 16, 19
    outdoor play and, 32
Process focus, in free play, 5
Proprioceptive sense, 24–25

Rabbits and 'Roos (game), 27
Race to the Top, 61–62
Ranger Rick magazine, 44, 45
Ranheim, D., 91, 93
Rantala, T., 6
Ratey, John, 28, 29
Recess/breaks in schools, 30, 31, 33–34, 37–38, 49
Resilience, 49, 64
Reverse Tag (game), 59
Ring Toss (game), 36
Risky play, 46–53
    benefits of, 48–50
    categories of, 50
    defined, 46
    educator role in, 50–51
    fear/safety concerns and, 46–48
    gender and, 47, 48, 51
    parents and, 46–48, 50–51, 52–53
    putting theory into practice, 50–51
    recommended resources, 52–53
    resilience and, 49
    risks vs. hazards and, 47
    rough-and-tumble play as, 50. *See also* Rough-and-tumble play
Rivkin, M. S., 41–42
Rochman, B., 33
Role-playing. *See* Dramatic play
Rorem, A., 62
Rotate It (game), 81–82
Rough-and-tumble play, 50, 54–60
    age and, 54–55
    educator role in, 56–59
    encouraging, 57–58
    fear/safety concerns and, 56–57, 59–60
    games in, 58–59
    gender and, 55–58, 59, 60
    health-related fitness factors and, 56
    nature of, 54–55
    parents and, 56–57, 59–60
    putting theory into practice, 56–59
    recommended resources, 59–60
    rules in, 56–57
    superhero play, 9, 59, 72–73, 74–75
    war and gun play, 54, 59, 72–73, 74–75
Rubin, K., 84
Rusty's Outdoor Loose Parts List, 93–94

Safety. *See* Fear/safety concerns
Sahlberg, Pasi, 10, 29, 33, 34, 61
Salinas-Gonzalez, I., 71, 74
Sampish, Allison, 82–83
Sampson, Scott, 41
Sandseter, Ellen Beate Hansen, 46, 50, 56
Save Our Schools, 37
Scaffolding
    construction play and, 86
    free play and, 9
    guided play and, 14, 17
Schein, D., 41–42
Science concepts
    construction play and, 85
    loose parts play and, 90, 93
Science Daily, 41
Scientific American, 12
Screen time
    construction play vs., 84
    fine motor play and, 76
    free play vs., 9, 10
    lack of physical contact and, 56
    myopia (nearsightedness) and, 32, 38
    nature play vs., 39
    outdoor play vs., 31, 32
    rough-and-tumble play vs., 56
See My Hands (game), 80–81

Self-knowledge, free play and, 7
Self-regulation
  cooperative play and, 64–65
  dramatic play and, 72
  free play and, 10–12
  guided play and, 15
Sensory development
  in big body play, 24–25
  in free play, 8
  in loose parts play, 90
  myopia (nearsightedness) and outdoor play, 32, 38
  in nature play, 40, 42, 43, 45
  in outdoor play, 35
September 11, 2001 terrorist attacks, 84–85
Serious Fun (Masterson & Bohart), 20
Sesame Street (television program), 64
Shadow Game, 68
Shadow Tag (game), 35, 58
SHAPE America (Society of Health and Physical Educators), 23, 28
Shrinking Room (game), 17–18
Simon Says (game), 19–20
Skenazy, Lenore, 37, 47, 48, 52
Skylar, H., 63
Sledding, 47, 50
Smart Moves (Hannaford), 28
Social-emotional development
  big body play and, 25, 26
  dramatic play and, 71–72, 75
  free play and, 11
  nature play and, 41
  outdoor play and, 32–33
  touch and, 56, 59
Social skills
  cooperative play and, 65–66
  dramatic play and, 71
  free play and, 7, 8
  outdoor play and, 32, 33–34
Social studies concepts
  guided play and, 15
  loose parts play and, 91
Sociodramatic play. *See* Dramatic play
Sole-Smith, V., 72
Spark (Ratey), 28, 29

Spark a Revolution in Early Education (Pica), 4
Sports
  play vs., 2, 5
  risky play injuries vs. sports injuries, 53
Statues (game)
  in guided play, 13, 14–15
  in outdoor play, 35
Stewart, Deborah, 82–83
Storli, R., 54–56
Strauss, V., 25
Stress
  among early childhood educators and, 2–3
  decline of play in children and, 2
  nature play and relaxation, 41
  overscheduling and, 2, 23, 30, 39
  recess/breaks in reducing, 30, 33, 34, 37–38
Suicide, lack of free play and, 7
Superhero play, 9, 59, 72–73, 74–75
Switcheroo (game), 68
Symbolic thinking, in loose parts play, 90

Tag games
  Blob Tag, 27, 58
  Elbow Tag, 58–59
  Reverse Tag, 59
  Shadow Tag, 35, 58
  Turtle Tag, 58
Tannock, M. T., 72, 73
Tate Sullivan, E., 3
Technology. *See* Science concepts; Screen time
Temple University, 20–21
This Is My Friend (game), 67
Topal, Cathy Weisman, 94
Touch It (game), 26–27, 43
Treasure hunts, 35, 44
Turtle Tag (game), 58

Under Deadman's Skin (Katch), 75
United Kingdom, research on outdoor play, 30, 32
University of Cambridge, 15–16

University of Tasmania, research on nature play, 39
University of Virginia, 62

Vandenberg, B., 84
Verbal mapping, in dramatic play, 71
Vestibular sense, 24–25
Vines, P., 23
Vision, myopia (nearsightedness) and, 32, 38
Vitamin D, outdoor play and, 32

Wang, M. L., 53
Wardle, F., 86–87
War play, 54, 59, 72–73, 74–75

The War Play Dilemma (Levin & Carlsson-Paige), 75
Weaver, M., 76
Weisberg, D. S., 13
A Whole New Mind (Pink), 10
Willis, Judy, 6
Wonder, authentic learning and, 39
Worth, S., 89
Wright, Charlotte Anne, 4, 20–21
Writing. *See also* Emergent literacy
  fine motor skills and, 76–83
Writing in Space (game), 82
Wunderled, 11

Zoss, J. M., 13

About the Author

Rae Pica is on a mission to ensure that children have the chance to be children and that child development guides all our practices with them. A consultant in early childhood education for more than 4 decades, Rae has served as a keynote speaker, workshop leader, and online course creator. She is the author of 23 books, including *What If Everybody Understood Child Development?* and *Spark a Revolution in Early Education: Speaking Up for Ourselves and the Children.* She has shared her expertise with such groups as the Centers for Disease Control and Prevention, the Head Start Bureau, the National Association for the Education of Young Children, and the *Sesame Street* Research Department. You can learn more about Rae and her work at www.raepica.com.